150
somewhat
iffy
poems

150
somewhat
iffy
poems

mike krabal

ISBN-10: 0-9975800-1-1
ISBN-13: 978-0-9975800-1-3

Contents

Judge This Book

Please judge this book by its cover.
Please pass judgement, then open and discover
An open invitation to your imagination,
And know that I'm open to open interpretation.
And know that I thank you for opening
The paper gateway to what's beneath,
To what's been waiting eagerly for you to read,
To poems longing for the eyes they need,
To poems friendly and fiery, stoked and burning,
All wrapped by a cover and expressed in writing,
And coming to life in minds when inciting
The urge to explore and roam freely
On wide-open ranges of boundless possibility.
Through pastures of poems brand new and unknown,
From a world of thought with a look of its own.
The view from inside are words juggling as rhymes
Then a door opens directly, and through it I find
The next poem I want to share with you
That's bizarre, reflective, about Mars and the stars,
Old cars, work, traveling, animals, or bars,
Late-night fun, when the world is right,
Or social issues when the world is wrong.
The next poem could be three lines or three pages long.
That's how the ones in this book seem to be,
An array of subjects from ornery to comedy,
And iffy in nature, and maybe in quality,
That is, if you're versed in poetry more than me.
But don't take them too seriously,
And have a laugh because once it's all over
You'll discover just another cover
Waiting on the back.

Dog Doo

I'm late for work. Let's get this going.
Come on, let's get the nuggets flowing.
There's no time for what you're doing.
Please hold still and save your moves,
Your squat and shuffle, your poopy prance,
Your here-and-there indecisive stance,
Your one, two, three look around.
Hooray...
You've found something on the ground.
Why the circles? Why the scooting?
What's distracting you from pooping?

Señor Sombrero

Once an old man named Señor Sombrero
Wore the largest hat in all of Mexico.
When the sun shone hot, it cast a great shadow.
Some say it covered him from his head to his toes,
And there were two holes poked through so
He could see where he goes.
Then one day, in a big field near Dormido,
He was harvesting poblanos
When all of a sudden, there came a tornado.
He looked and found no shelter to stow,
And, at eighty-one, he was old and slow,
So he squatted down as low as he could go,
Hiding beneath his great sombrero.
In came the wind, and he hovered to and fro,
But when the tornado finally swallowed him whole,
He flew into the sky just like a crow.
Señor Sombrero was the first UFO.

Bizarre Attraction

Insofar as it can be seen,
The bizarre is most attracting.
Grabbing eyes from afar,
Trancelike gaze, and there you are
Witnessing a sight most frightening,
A man sizzled, struck by lightning.

A black, hollow shadow
Following a peripheral path.
Your head swivels upon your neck,
Allowing your eyes a focused check.
What was that, that arrested your chest?
Your heart's pounding
From a fleeting glimpse.

It's not polite to stare.
Dare to aim it away from there.
A sight unlike any other,
An impossible connection between two brothers.
They're a Siamese set that's accepted their form
And find it to be their comfortable norm,
But for you, it's freakishly new,
Seeing this one being that's really two.

Still, there's another dimension undefined,
Found in hallucinogens for the mind
Where color collages and chemical massages
Barrage your brain and edit reality.
Discover an altered montage of life
And experience duality
And satisfaction as you absorb
Another bizarre attraction.

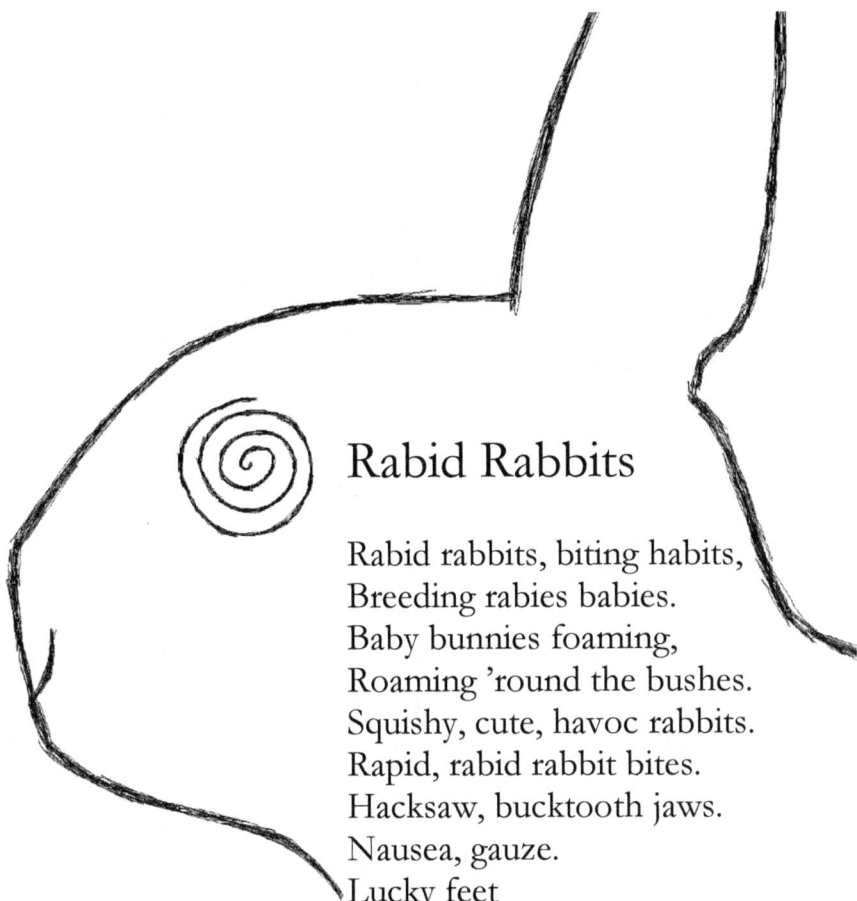

Rabid Rabbits

Rabid rabbits, biting habits,
Breeding rabies babies.
Baby bunnies foaming,
Roaming 'round the bushes.
Squishy, cute, havoc rabbits.
Rapid, rabid rabbit bites.
Hacksaw, bucktooth jaws.
Nausea, gauze.
Lucky feet
No more.

Long ears hear fear.
Fiery, wiry eyes twitching,
Glitching, direction-switching
Army of varmints, razor teeth
Meaty treat, mushy brained,
Strange, deranged, manged,
Insane, evil rabbits
Beware.
Lucky feet
No more.

My Temple

My body, my temple? My ass!
It's not that simple.
First, there's the pimples.
They're everywhere, on my face and legs,
Beneath my hair on my back and arms
And even down…there.

And speaking of hair,
Where did it go? Where oh where?
It's not on my head.
Now, up there's a glare.

Then there's the fat.
What am I ever to do with that?
Diet? Lipo? I've always been fat.
It'll come back.

And how about my miserable skin?
Do you see the condition it's in?
There's a rainbow of rashes
From my chin to my shin.

Do I even have to mention my height?
I'd like to at least be in your line of sight.
Five foot something would be all right.

Oh, my dreaded eyes,
They're the size of raisins.
These glasses barely help my vision.
And they chase away women
With their inch-thick lenses.

And let me not forget, I generally smell.
I sweat so bad, can't you tell?
I have B.O. from head to toe.
Bad enough to sting your nose.

My body, my temple, is a bunch of trash.
I feel better when I live life fast.
Since these genetics are going to last,
I'm going hard until I crash.

Unentitled American

Unentitled Americans exist.
They were raised by poor parents,
And their large inheritance
Wasn't wealth, but discipline.
They respect their elders.
And, when spoken to, they listen.
Indeed, there are unentitled American citizens.

They played in the dirt as children.
They're familiar with tools and building.
Towards hard work, they're more than willing.
They know struggle firsthand,
And aren't afraid to take a stand.
They give to their fellow man.
Unentitled American citizens love this land.

Their mouths aren't familiar with a silver spoon.
Toward helplessness, they're immune.
Toward honesty, they're in tune.
Toward a lie, they won't give it credit.
The saying, "All Americans are entitled" is bullshit.
Need some proof they exist?
An unentitled American citizen has written this.

Childhood

The only part of life I understood
Was the wonderful time called childhood.
Pretending was on center stage.
Growing taboo with age.
Curiosity's clout was carried to the clouds.
There was nothing I didn't want to figure out.
Nothing was beyond the realm of imagination,
And every lucid vision could reach manifestation.
I could be a cop one day and a robber the next.
Being both in one day was the best.
Yes, the world worked differently then.
Value came in a very best friend.
Someone to share your deepest secrets
And the first glimpse of the new.
Someone to help make sense of it all, as you grew.
Best friends are still valued,
So is shared time,
Now most of my time is shared with my employer,
And that's how I'm defined.
Life as an adult is so confined.
Constant tests aid in the formation of stress.
I would feel blessed if not so pressed.
Freedom to use my imagination is still there,
But I'm tired from work and just don't care.
A good night's sleep and a nap brings a smile.
I miss the days of energy for miles.
Those were the days that I've grown to adore.
How I wish I could go back
For just a few more.

Anxiety

I don't want to talk to you.
What exactly do you do?
Excuse me.
Was that a joke about me?
It wasn't funny.
Wait.
What was that behind me?
I can't see in front of me.
What's that running?
Oh no! It's coming.
Or is it?
I hope it isn't.
If it is, I might go missing.
I can't see anything.
I'm losing my vision.
Getting it checked is so expensive.
I don't have the money.
Doctors make me feel funny,
And white coats scare me.
Are you staring at me?
Is something on my face?
I know I'm being watched.
I wish they'd stop.
Last night I was locked
In a box on a spaceship
With aliens flying it.
They're real, stop denying.
You gotta believe me!

I'm not lying!
I'm not crazy!
My heart's racing!
You don't know what I'm facing.
There are secret societies!
They're trying to find me!
I've been in hiding!
Did you hear that?
What was that sound?
They're all around
I need to sit down.
You're freaking me out!
Did you hear what I said?
There's a chip in my head!
There's a chip in my head!
We're all gonna be dead!
We're all gonna be dead!
I'm so itchy!
Bugs are all over me!
Bugs are inside of me!
You gotta believe me!
You gotta believe me!
Hey, why are you leaving?
Don't question my sobriety.
I don't have anxiety.

Plastic pieces assembled with speed,
Built on a platform of building cheap,
Shipped to foreigners overseas,
China, turn away some business, please.
You're an enabler to our economy,
And what you make, we barely need.
We've got junk up to our knees
That we need like we need disease.

Made in
China

money

junk

With credit cards we've been hoarding
The sort of stuff not worth sorting.
We're a nation bent on absorbing
Great gobs of goods all affordably,
Much, much cheaper than they use to be,
Worthless things to you and me.
We're consuming more quarterly
Than what's called for, decent, or orderly.

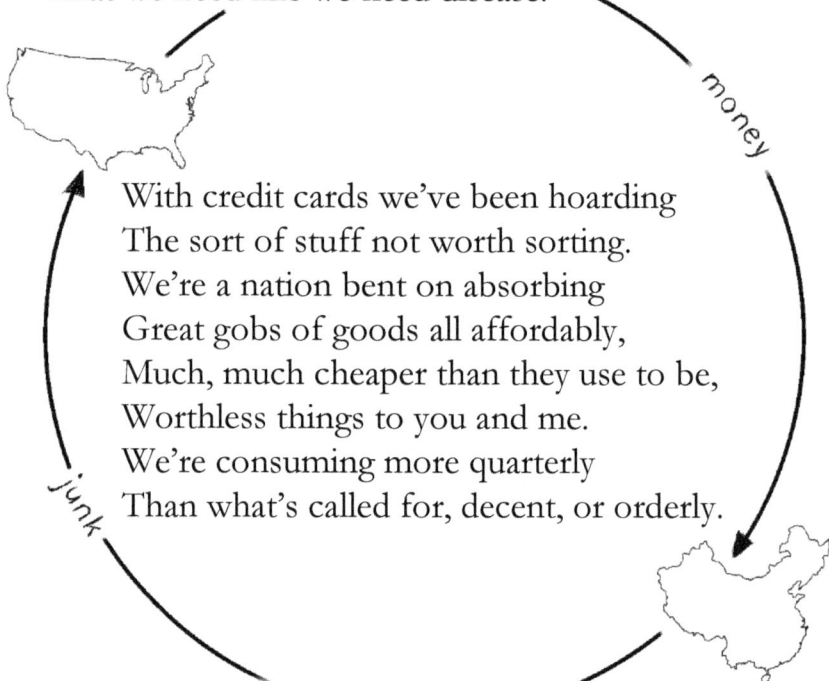

A country once great, now an addict.
We're thirsty, like gotta have it.
China the dealer, feeding the habit.
We're sickened spenders, money rabid,
Buying bargain plastic bunny rabbits.
Cut the cord, China. Let us have it.
We'll survive and recover rapid.
Got to stop the spending madness.

There must be a way to make sure
Certain things don't linger.
A path toward and end
Where no one wants to follow
There's no glory held in the lifeless
Body of a corpse,
Dead and hollow.

Corpse

It's a leftover, a physical imprint
Evidence that consciousness
Was once animated within
It's now useless, dead weight
Decaying into another form
When years of growth
Passed before this final state.

Is it even a body anymore,
Or solely a part of nature?
Where its value is in nutrient richness.
For the living, it's immensely undesired,
Offensive in smell and company,
Utterly useless in progress,
Totally expired.

If given a voice and a few words of finality
The corpse might say
With great, haunting labor,

"Please move on. I'm through here.
 There's nothing more to attend to.
    With every trick I have left,
        I must repel you."

Old Sayings

Old sayings
Will outlast
You and me.
Just wait
And see.

I must get out of this relationship.
It's always pulling me back.
I don't look like I used to.
And I've always felt I could rely on you,
But you let me down,
And I need to stand my ground.
I need to put you down,
And hold my head high,
And ask myself why
I can't get enough.
It's not healthy to live like this.
Oh, this relationship with potato chips.

Can't Get Enough

Bigfoot, ghosts, favorite numbers, skeptical suspicion,
Does credibility ever coincide with superstition?
Or is it all driven by fleeting intuition?
Some seek proof, the truth; they petition.

The
Paranormal

Faint feeling, an electrical emission,
But where is it exactly, and what's its composition?
Paranormal energy from another dimension?
An enigmatic being that defies definition?

Wait a second! Was that an apparition,
Going through another stage of human life, a transition?
Well, isn't that an absurd proposition,
Handed down through religion and tradition?

Certainly, the universe is powered by no magician.
To believe that you'd express a mental condition.
How can we know without returning from death's partition,
If a further state of life exists with cognition?

So, maybe there's an afterlife after all, a spiritual position.
But how can that be proved without opposition?
The argument will linger on, verbal ammunition,
Cycling forever, true or false, endless repetition.

So many answers elude recognition.
And experts like statisticians and technicians
Show little interest in research through enchanted missions.
So, we're left with well-meaning but amateur expeditions.

Wishful explorers reach conclusions without inhibition,
Passionately fueled by unwavering volition,
Expressing opinions that breed contradiction,
The very foundation of the paranormal condition.

Milk

White skin gleaming bright.
Glow in the dark,
Day and night.
Sunshine, awesome light.
Boy, that skin is really white.

Applying lotion by the ocean.
Thick and creamy,
Rapid motion.
Sunshine, awesome light.
Sunblock, that skin's so white.

Freckles, burns, blisters—yikes.
Seeking fun,
I rent a bike.
Sunshine, awesome light.
Good lord, that skin's really white.

Cool guys, tan and built.
I ride by.
They yell, "Milk."
Sunshine, awesome light.
That's life with skin so white.

Break Out

I'm allergic to alcohol.
When I drink, I break out in dancing,
And everything's funny.
My mouth won't stop running,
And I feel stunning and cunning.
I blow money like the wind,
And I'm everyone's friend.
I'll tell you a story.
Then I tell you again.
I forget what I'm saying,
And forget what I'm doing
As my grip loosens
On the drinks I'm spilling.
Then I stop listening,
And my ears stop working,
And my wiener starts thinking.
That's why I'm allergic to alcohol.
And that's why I quit drinking.

Texas

The state line here is hard to find.
With nine hundred miles of friendly inside,
Someone will help you around.
Texans are grounded.
A warm blend of spice and nice,
They're aware of the good life.
They're heavily defined and western refined.
Texas doesn't go on forever, but surely tries.
It tries like the men of the Alamo.
They didn't give up.
Not 'til all were counted.
And Texas won't give up on you.
And you can count on that.

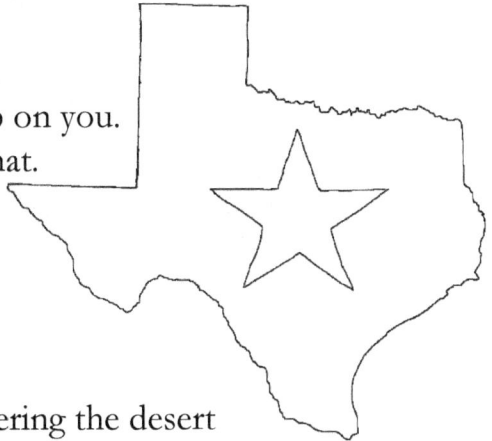

I obliged my welcome,
And spent a week wandering the desert
Down by Mexico. Out there to clear my mind,
To fill my eyes with the night sky over Big Bend.
There's treasure there in the sunsets and wind.
I followed the long-range views to the wide plains
In the heart of this land, to the pine forests
And beaches of the east.
I've discovered that such a place is worthy of a legend.
Though, I never did truly come to know
If anything's any bigger here,
God knows a breath of air in Texas
Fills my lungs and swells my heart so
That I find myself more than I was.

Little Miss Lincoln

Four score
And seven years ago,
I met a girl
Down in Tupelo,
With hair on her face,
That got me thinking,
"Man, she looked just like
Abe Lincoln."

Employer, Employer: Soul Destroyer

Take off your coat and stay.
We have a great 401k.
Benefits the very first day.
Repetitiveness is our way.

Have a taste of security.
Pay with your serenity.
Stifle all creativity.
Drown natural positivity.

Only one year until vacation.
Then fifty-one weeks of deprivation.
Embrace it with elation.
Doesn't this sound great, son?

Invite a friend, get a reward.
Invite them to come and be bored.
Thirty years of this in store.
Why retire? Have some more.

My Girlfriend's Burqa

My girlfriend's burqa has changed my life.
It's saved me from a bunch of fights.
Before, she'd dress in stuff so tight
I refused to take her out at night.

She was the definition of eye candy,
All sexy dressed in skirts real scanty,
Makeup on and looking fancy,
Luring in drunks when dancing.

Some guy would always test my limit.
Mess with her instead of other women.
Fights were possible at any minute.
I never cared to be caught up in it.

Now my life is so blessed.
No more dealing with that mess.
I love that burqa. It's the best.
Soothes my mind, fixed my stress.

Crash and Burn

Crash and burn.
That's how you learn.
Experience is earned,
Not deserved,
Not easily served.
It only occurs
With effort.
Crashing may hurt.
You might flirt
With disaster at first,
But stay alert
And convert
The sweat and the dirt,
The passion that burns,
Your energy that yearns
Into your work,
And in turn,
You'll have learned.

First Slice

If you were a girl,
I'd name you Lisa,
And love you forever,
My dearest pizza.

Age and Pain

Age and Pain,
Two companions
Better unmet.
Even mosquitos
Go away for a bit.
Sunburns, they come and go.
Chickenpox
Pop up once in life.
A heartbreak might happen
Once or twice.
But Age and Pain,
They're not going away.
Only growing closer
Every day.

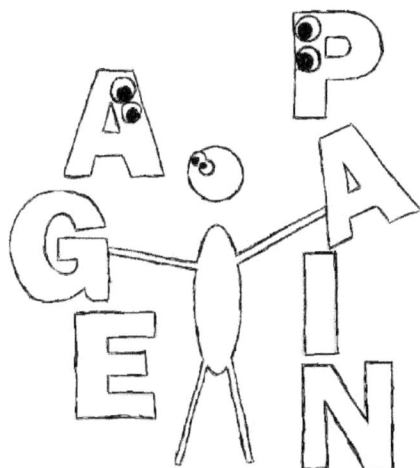

Asian Pain

I don't know
A thang
About
Asian Pain.

Moody Weather

Deep purple clouds weigh upon the sky.
Marching in, thick with wind,
Matched with rain,
If so possible,
They'd bring pain.

Six strikes of lightning.
Anxiety ascends a ladder steep,
To the top, far too high, far too unstable,
Another rung. Another strike.
This is frightening.

Walled in, closed in, wait it out.
What's next? What was that?
Thrash, slash,
The sky wails.
Uncertainty fuels doubt.

On, the storm boils,
Raging over the rim of a high pot.
Angry with elements quick to leave behind.
At its mercy, it demands I remember,
Stealing space inside my mind.

I Want to Laugh

I need more funny
More than I need more money.
I need to cackle like a jackal
Until my voice crackles
And my Adam's apple rattles.
I need laughter that a rafter would be after,
With water-gushing eye geysers
Spraying so hard I baptize flies as they fly by.
I need to hear more jokes
Where I laugh so hard I sprain my throat.
I need more funny like a bee needs honey.
Like sticky laughing fits
Sticking with me 'til my wit's end.
Ending with me laughing again and again
Like I like to laugh at someone
Who keeps cutting wind.
Oh please stop.
I wanna wheeze 'til I drop
Until snot rockets out of my nostril slots.
I want to crack up
Until my teeth fall out
And my tongue falls off,
Until I can't talk,
And I can't remember,
What gender Bruce Jenner is,
Or if he surrendered,
His member to a blender,
Last December.

I want to laugh
Like I want to laugh
At a giraffe with a short neck,
Like I'm insane with a pet Great Dane
That I gave my name,
Mike the Great Dane.
I want to laugh,
As I feed him snacks,
And he quacks,
But Mike the Great Dane
Ain't a duck.
I want to laugh,
And laugh,
And laugh,
Until I've had enough.

Awkward Guy

"Pardon me. You have beautiful eyes."
That's not a compliment from the awkward guy.
"I like your eyeballs, girl.
Why don't you give them a whirl?"
Now, that's what the awkward guy might say,
Boldly serious, in the middle of the day.
In the wrong place, at the wrong time.
There's really no reason to his awful rhymes.
He's confused and socially complicated,
Hardly welcome, but not really hated.
His presence is unwanted the longer he lingers,
Especially when he begs, "Pull my finger."
He never fails to foul a situation,
When he cuts in mid-conversation.
He's aware of his rudeness, as well turned off,
But tries to interact without being lost.
Then, just when things seem to be going his way,
He'll feel inspired, raise his voice, and say,
"Can I? Do you? Would? Uh, want to later today?
Do you want? Can I take you to lunch later?"
Good grief, man! Get a translator!
A sympathetic gal will agree, uncompelled,
Knowing lunch will not go well.

The Probe

I'm already worried about the 40-something probe,
And I've got more than a decade to go.
A finger's never lingered near there before.
I'm scared to death for what's in store.

Soon some doctor will take a look at me,
And violate my most private privacy.
I can't live with that happening,
So I'm going to try a different thing.

Since there's a few years until it's my turn,
I'll take it upon myself to read and learn.
Then when it's time for the probe,
I'll put a glove on and give it a go.

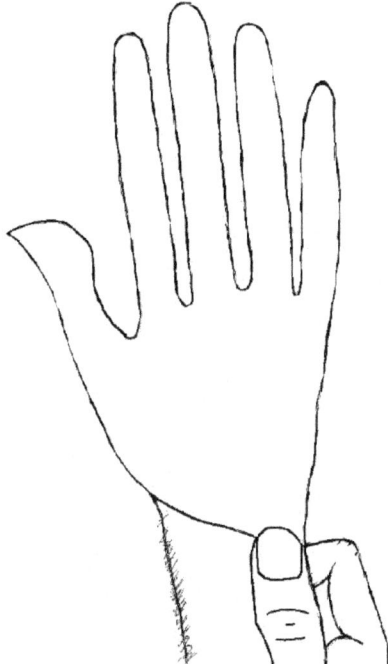

Watch This

Hey, watch this!
I stand high and raise a fist.
I'm going for it!
This is gonna be legit.

They've never seen anything like this.
I have to fully commit,
And they'll have to admit
That I'm the shit.

I know I can pull this off.
It's really not that high, this loft.
And there's a couch below that's soft.
But I've never jumped from something so tall.

There's no room for doubt,
And they're beginning to shout.
My legs aren't feeling so stout.
They'll never let me back out.

Okay, this will be easy as pie.
I'm not scared. I'm not that guy.
On three, I'm ready to fly.
One, two. Oh my, it's so high!

Stop thinking about a broken limb.
Stop thinking about a smashed shin.
Come on, man, this isn't the end.
Okay, on three, again.

Count of one, I'm looking low.
Count of two, I'm moving slow.
Count of three, here I go.
I'm in the air—oh, no, no, no!

Someone help! I came up short!
Missed the couch and hit the floor!
My foot's in pain! Something's torn!
It hurts bad! It's more than sore!

And it's cranked in a weird angle!
Oh crap, it's so freaking mangled!
I can't move it. Look at it dangle!
That wasn't worth a broken ankle.

I Wonder

I wonder if I've lost my wonder.
Another year's tucked in my belt, deep under.
It's been a while since I've gone beyond yonder.
It's been a while since I've wandered.

I wonder if I'm still struck by the thunder
Of a coming storm, brewing stronger.
It's been a while since I ran for cover,
And vulnerability, I have pondered.

I wonder if age has taken my wonder?
As a child, I wandered and wondered.
Here and there, over and under.
Never far from something to discover.

In place, now, change is my only wonder.
As it happens, it brings discomfort.
Much more so than when I was younger.
When I was different by years in number.

Now, often before my night's slumber
I lay and wonder if I leave to wander,
Can I be caught again in the spell I was under
When I was under the spell of wonder?

Catchy

There's a tune in my head.
I can't get rid of it.
Last night, I took it to bed.
This morning, it was back again.

In my head, it's hovering,
Lingering, and covering thoughts
When I'd rather think
Of other things.

It's predatory in its stalking
Even when I'm walking,
Even when I'm talking.
And, it's silly, of all things.

It's poking, prodding,
Popping, and playing,
Repetitively restarting,
With great power in staying.

How can I chase it away?
I could use a distraction.
What's that on the radio?
Oh, that sounds catchy...

Foolish

The most foolish one here
Is not the beast of inadequate brain
But the one who fouls his home,
Who renders the environment lame.

Hungry Thoughts

All those things I should have said
Are still alive inside my head.
They're constant haunts and recurring,
Regretfully reminding, always stirring.
In the night, they rise to power,
Feeding on the quiet minutes
Of the darkest hours.

Lot Lizard

Her hair's dark and shiny with really long bangs.
A light tap on my truck says she wants to get paid.
It's awfully cold out, and she's a fine little honey.
I invite her inside knowing she wants money.

So far, so good. Her dress is tight and she's thin.
That's a bonus, and might be a win.
Her butt's nice and round and sticks out a mile.
I really like what I see, and crack a big smile.

She's dressed for the cold, but I see a little lace.
She's being shy and hiding her face.
She speaks up with a whisper. She's got a bad lisp.
If I didn't know better, that sounded like a hiss.

Her shiny, black gloves lift handcuffs from her purse.
She's ready to play, and I'm ready for her.
But I still haven't seen her hiding eyes.
Her long, dark bangs have been a disguise.

I tell her to slide on over and get a little closer.
She brings the cuffs, and when we're shoulder to shoulder,
She whispers, "Hold these, baby. It's about to get real."
I reach for them, and she cuffs me to the wheel.

That sneaky whore just tricked me!
What's next, a robbery?
I have to keep cool and take control.
She speaks up, "Sorry. I don't want you to go."

I tell her, "Look, I wasn't planning to leave just yet."
She replies, "Most men do and you will, I bet."
She removes her coat, revealing a tight shirt and small breasts.
She says, "I'm lonely, please promise you'll want this?"

I say, "Sure. I promise" seeing no other way out.
She says, "Now you'll find out what I'm talking about."
She parts her hair and her face appears.
I cry out for my life! I'm drowning in fear!

I yell, "What the hell are you? Get away from me!"
Her wig flies off as she's startled by my shrieks.
She's fully revealed and I scream, "Lizard, lizard!"
She looks like a black magic accident from an evil wizard.

She has the lips of an iguana! Oh, the drama!
And long, pointed teeth looking ready for trauma.
And her bulging ass in those tight pants
Was a rolled-up tail, I missed at first glance.

Her lizard eyes are moving in different directions.
I notice she's avoiding the mirror's reflection.
Her skin is pale green, something's drastically wrong.
And, oh God, her tongue, it's a foot long!

She scrambles for her coat, her bag, and her wig.
I'm yanking on the cuffs and hanging out of my rig.
I'm trying to break free, but it ain't working.
I can't escape, and my wrist is hurting.

She begins weeping, and seems more scared than me.
She's now dressed and cowering in the seat.
She says, "Don't be scared. Please don't leave.
I'm desperate, lonely, and want some company."

I calm, knowing I'm not going to die.
She's pleading for me to close the door and join her inside.
My mind is racing and I feel like I'm dreaming.
How could a lizard woman be sitting beside me?

She scoots closer and unlatches the cuffs.
I bolt out the door and begin to run.
Then I'm stopped dead in my tracks by a tug.
She's pulling me back with her enormous tongue.

There's no escaping her now. I'm back in the truck,
Back in my seat, and shit out of luck.
I'm completely powerless and utterly stuck
With a lizard woman who just wants to get paid.

Now there's no one in sight and she's coming on to me.
Her cold blood is heating up. She's suddenly horny.
She just leaped on my lap without any warning.
I'm afraid she might take me forcefully.

But then a thought crosses my mind that's rather vile,
And it's mixed with the thought, "It's been a while."
I tell her directly, "This night's gonna be wild."
She cracks a knowing crocodile smile.

I'll have one hell of a story in the long run.
No one will believe it, but telling it will be fun.
Heck, I might even miss her when she's gone,
But for now, I have to do what has to be done.

Itsy Bitsy

The itsy-bitsy spider
Is now an itsy-bitsy splatter
For scaring me so bad
That I released my bladder.

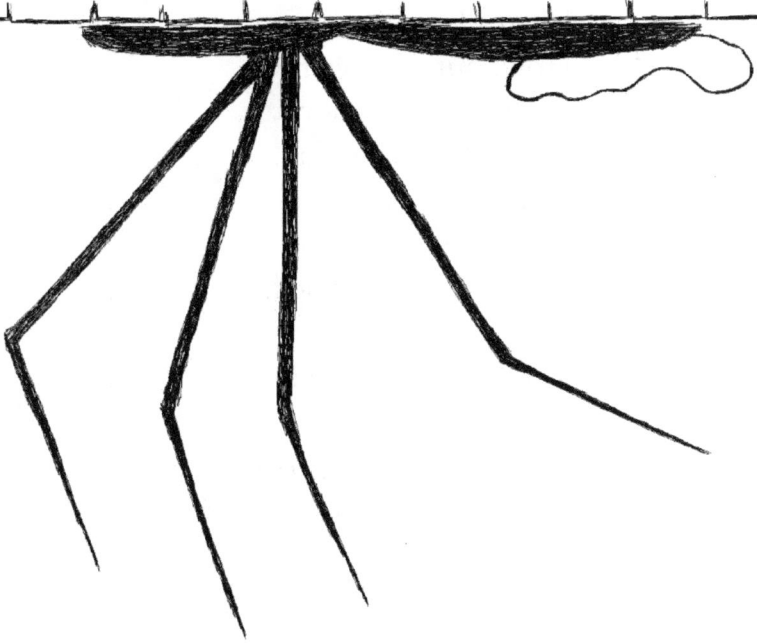

Don't Look

It's really not fair
How, out of anywhere,
Time passes so slow
During the workday.
It doesn't care
And is quick to dare
A glance at the clock.
Tick-tock, a stare.
The hands of the clock
Go nowhere.
Now I know it's possible
For time to stop.

Grandma's Glue

Our family,
Our family, you see,
We're not what we used to be.
Our greatest part was our matriarch.
Now there's not much left since she left.

Of course, we lost our patriarch too,
But Grandma, she was the glue.
Sure, we miss Grandpa, and loved him too.
He went first, but he lived on,
Through Grandma until she was called home.

Still we linger, but barely together.
Holidays now seem like just-another days,
Where our ways just aren't the same.
We reminisce about the good old days,
With Christmases packed with family from far away.

Time has passed and now heads are graying.
Children then, are parents now,
Parents who watch their children play,
While generations become their own.
Holidays keep us close to home.

Families grow from the seeds sown.
Grandparents are made from children long ago,
Matriarchs and patriarchs of their own,
Holding everyone together, heading a family,
Visited by grandchildren, becoming the glue.

'Til Death Do US Part

To this life, I thee wed.
I promise I'll always do my best.
My grace, to you, I will give.
I'll do no less than fully live.

I'll not dismiss this precious chance,
And with risk and fate I'll choose to dance.
There's no reward in the bland.
The Golden Rule will be my brand.

Each day's brilliant sun
Shines out possibilities by the ton.
I will grab them and I will run
With your wind until I'm done.

Life, this I promise unto thee.
To make the most, most certainly,
Love, smile, and help faithfully,
Until I submit all energy.

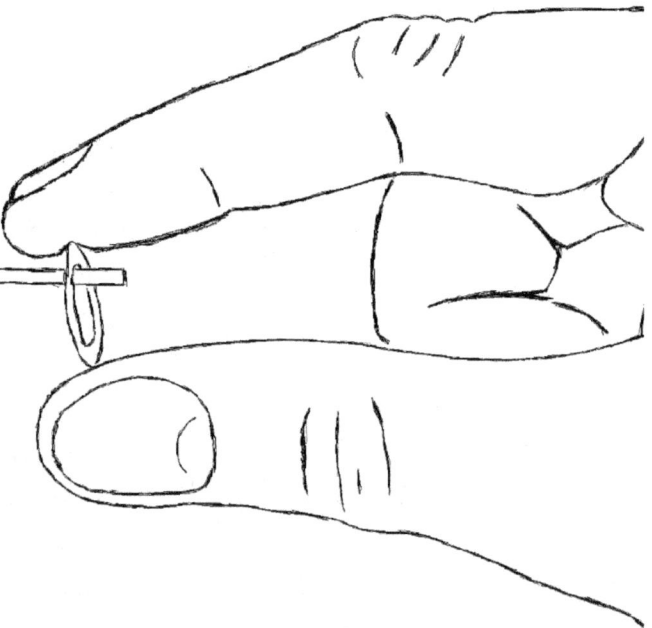

Writer's Block

Blank sheet.
Writer's block.
A writing virus has been caught.
Internally infecting,
Intimidating space invading the brain.
Brightly blinding,
With square inches of white so bright
A writer is mired in white noise
When finding even a letter
To introduce with ink or pencil.
Why can't these ideas come pre-stenciled?
Trace them to the finish line.
Line for line predefined.
Effort absent from the mind.
A cure for writer's block,
We'll never find.
But there's a treatment
In endlessly trying.

Never Ever

Never should it be made
Ever aware
Your wife is having
A day of bad hair.

The Lottery

Please, please, please, please let me win!
I'd give a pinky, a toe, a pinky toe to win.
To whom it may concern in the universe we're in:
Please, please, please, please let me win!
I'd be more grateful than anyone on Earth,
If I could just taste that outrageous net worth.
I'd be so charitable you'd have to stop me.
You'd literally have to cuff me and drop me.
I'd help so many with all of that money.
It would pour on the poor like fountains of honey.

Please, please, please, please let me win!
I'd give a kidney, no problem.
Are you kidding me?
The things I could do to help my family,
Easing their stress and gifting them randomly.
I'd share it to build a stronger community.
Money's not all evil if used for unity.
There'd be no more hours of forced boredom,
No more days of labor and false conforming,
No more stiffing friends when I can't afford it,
And I'd finally have a car in good working order.
To whom it may concern in the universe we're in:
Please, please, please, PLEASE let me win!

47

Cardiac Paranoia

Eyes in the skies. French fry saucer flies by.
Fast food plotting, pulling me inside.
Burgers and fries. It's all lies!

Fake food fast. Factory burger meat.
Pesticide planters giving me cancer.
Burgers and fries in disguise.

No escape from the great taste.
Salty sweet treats begging me to eat.
Burgers and fries, no allies.

Fat additives, fats cells added, belly padded,
Deep-fried breakfast keeping me alive.
Burgers and fries, greasy sunrise.

Soft drink sweet, carbonated dirty bomb.
Sugary fluids, health ruined.
Burgers and fries, blood pressure rise.

Creeping hunger overtaking my mind.
Fish on a hook, order large size.
Burgers and fries one more try.

Heart pain, clogged vein,
Profit reigns, vision fades,
Burgers and fries, my demise.

Truth Be Told

Truth be told,
Being young
Never gets old.

Drink and Write

I drink and I write.
And if that's not right, I'll quit tonight.
Drinking I'll quit, and writing I'll stop.
I'll stop thinking of writing,
And drinking 'til dropping.
If writing isn't right amongst a drink,
I'll fight the urge to do what I think.
Decisions I make while drinking aren't right,
But writing while drinking is quite fun in the night.
Subjects of sin come in sight a bit brighter,
When writing while drinking in night's low light.
Lore, lust, and lurkers of the night
Bring life to words as I drink and write.
Dark skies inspire me to drink myself higher,
And write on the dire subjects of fear and liars,
Brimstone and fire.
I sweat from my brow, scowl and perspire,
And admire and record the choir,
Of ideas shouting from within before they expire,
Another shot of the heat, the whiskey burns hot.
Still, I desire to drink and write.
I shall not stop.

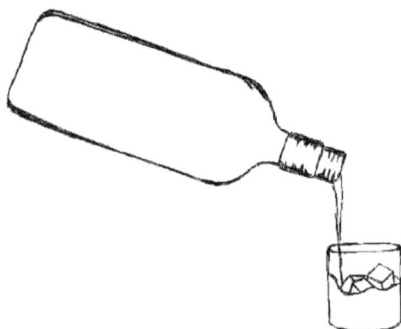

Late

Manhood is a train,
And I'm late to the station.
There's been a way to be a man since creation,
But I don't adhere or hear the call.
I'm lost in free fall.
Down and down. Up, up, and around.
Direction unknown,
A man run aground.
By now, I should've settled down
Like everyone else in this little town.
My girlfriend can't be my girlfriend forever,
But I can't afford a ring to give her.
Unknown potential, what's my calling?
I want to contribute, but I'm stalling.
These dead-end jobs stunt my growing.
It's frustrating not knowing
Where the future is going.

Neighbor's Dog

Dear sir or madam,

As your neighbor I'd rather not behave this way,
but to share in your ownership of a mouthy dog is
most unsavory. The neighborhood used to be calm.
We'd spend long evenings out on the lawn, and enjoy
our coffee on the deck at the crack of dawn. Now all
of that is gone.

So, I'm sure you'll not be offended tomorrow when
your peace is upended by what I have in store. You
see, I desire to fan the fire and find out if your dog's
bite has any fiber. I want to weed through its snarls
and snaps and theatrical gestures. I want to take your
mouthy mutt's measure. Is your dog a survivor? We'll
find out after dark when I'm in your yard releasing my
new pet tiger.

P.S. Best of luck to your mutt. Once and for all,
its mouth will be shut.

Onetime Lovers

Long and lean, but I sure ain't mean.
Come on, girl, you're the one I need.
I saw you over there looking at me.

Cowboy spying, I know you know
How a night like this is gonna go.
Take my hand and dance real slow.

I'll hold you tighter than a buckin' bull.
You're all mine when the moon is full.
It's too late to escape the pull.

This moment fate's been waiting on,
Late-night lovers, once before dawn.
In the morning, I'll be gone.

Dare to Cry Wolf

Wolf! You looked! What a laugh!
Wolf! You looked! How about that?
Just saying wolf makes you scared.
Mister, there's no wolf way out there.

Little boy, I wouldn't do that again if I were you.
See, I know the wolf and he knows me too.
Once I was a little guy just like you.
And the wolf nearly killed me, like he'll do.

Yes, I know the wolf, and the more you cry,
The closer you'll drawl him to your side.
His big teeth and evil eyes
Will surely catch you by surprise.

Listen, you don't know him like I do.
I know all the little boys he's eaten like you.
They had rosy cheeks and golden hair too.
Some he boiled in a pot of stew.

Some he yanked right out of bed.
Some he simply ripped to shreds.
Think of that tonight when you lay your head.
Think of those little boys filled with dread.

Hear their hearts pounding in their chests
When they were stirred from their rest
On the dark night that the evil wolf crept
Sight unseen to the side of their beds.

So, cry wolf again if you dare.
Aren't you a big boy? Are you scared?
You thought it was funny. You didn't care.
Have a look behind you. The wolf's right there!

Ha ha, little boy! Made you look!
Your face turned pale with fear of the wolf.
Your pride and bravery, I just took.
Now find something else to do. You're off the hook.

I would, mister, but you must turn around!
The wolf has crept upon you without a sound!
Little boy, stop that! I'll not turn 'round.
What do you take me for, a foolish clown?

You are foolish, mister. Listen to the kid.
I'm the wolf that never forgets.
You were lucky once, but that wasn't the end.
You've cried wolf for the last time, old friend.

Second Slice

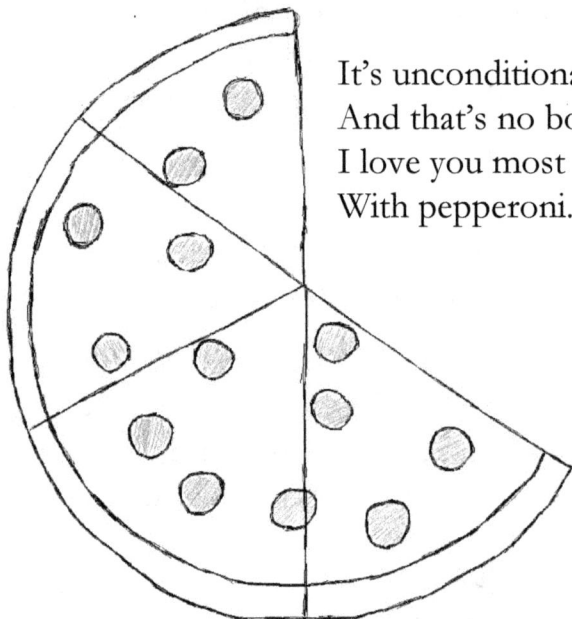

It's unconditional,
And that's no bologna.
I love you most
With pepperoni.

Gingers

Gingers like the sun,
But the sun's a devilish
Son of a gun.
Gunning for gingers.
Shooing and shunning
Us to the shadows.
To the world we know,
And to the world we show,
Our stunning white canvas of skin.
We hide from the light.
The sun's power and might,
With SPF we fight,
But we'll never win.

Birthdays

I've barely settled into this age,
And knocking on the door is my next birthday.
How fast they come without warning.
I woke up with crow's feet the other morning.
Actually, they had been with me quite a while,
Deep, identifying marks of a smile.
There is still light in my eyes, bright as the sun,
But crow's feet are rays of proof, and my youth is gone.

From years one to ten, don't we celebrate?
Then skip a few 'til we're teenaged,
Then skip again to sweet sixteen.
Next thing you know, aren't we driving?
And life speeds along, crossing eighteen and adulthood.
Twenty-one comes, we celebrate that life is good.
We accelerate, winding up at twenty-five,
And that happens in a blink of an eye.
Then we skip a plot of years counting by five.
Thirty's here, some say that's our prime.

Then the years really pick up steam.
Celebrating in tens, becomes our theme.
We celebrate the arrival of another decade.
A flood of time passes, age cascades.
Forty, fifty, sixty, finding ourselves seasoned well,
Finding aches and pains, and knees that went to hell.
Then a break from labor is on the horizon.
We can see the light of retirement.

And time meets friction then slightly slows.
We share our stories from long ago.
Another decade seems far away.
Hopes are high that it's a goal we'll make.
We do. We've survived like we always have.
Now other parts of our body are going bad.
Unlike our youth, we know our doctor by first name.
But, like our youth, with each new birthday,
We celebrate.

Soul Connection

Our whole connection,
Is a soul connection,
An old connection,
A story-told connection.
Now and then,
Through past lives,
With spirits aligned,
We've always arrived,
Together,
You and me,
Side by side.

Abs

Want six-pack abs, man?
Lucky for you, I have a plan.
Put on your tightest tee and follow me.
We're going to walk downtown.
Women will be all around.
The secret to this exercise,
Is looking good in their eyes.
Walk with me step for step.
Suck it in, and hold your breath,
Down this sidewalk and up the other.
We'll take a break in the alley later.
Okay, man, engage those abs, and hide that flab.
You'll be breaking a sweat before you know it.
You see, loose shirts are the enemy,
The way they hide the physiques,
Of guys like you and me.

Humanity

Humanity. Humanity. Oh, the humanity.
To understand it could spark insanity.
A phenomenal species beyond understanding.
Where do we begin?
How about with vanity?
Mirror, mirror, on the wall,
Who's afraid to admit their flaws?
Humanity. Humanity. Oh, it's humanity.
Mirror, mirror, tell me why,
We only take photos of our good side,
And an imperfect picture ruins our pride,
Everything's me, me, my, mine, all the time,
And we're not fine unless our ego's high.
Mirror, mirror, tell me why
We'd treat one another better
If we all were blind.

That's just the beginning. Now the rest.
Tell me who is Earth's only pest?
Humanity. Humanity. Oh, it's humanity.
Cross-pollinating across the blue planet.
Hindering the pollination of flowers.
Pollinating solely for money and power.
Powerfully turning our sweet home sour.
For thousands of years we knew balance.
That's changed with modern practice.
We worship a capitalist creed of greed,
Buying into false material needs,
From companies leading us as sheep.
So off track, it's hard to believe.

Humanity. Humanity. Dangerous humanity.
Natural-born killer, welcome to the world.
Your kind are in charge.
They're running loose, reckless, and at large.
Humanity is where all problems start,
So now we're strangers to nature,
And Mother Nature's in danger.
Poaching breeds anger.
Another bullet in the chamber.

Humanity. Humanity. Prolific humanity,
Will our numbers
Guarantee a future calamity?
Our population is rising.
We're always in season.
Forget about rabbits.
We're overbreeding.
And forget about natural laws.
Now everyone survives,
Not "only the strong."
We're exploiting this loophole,
But for how long?

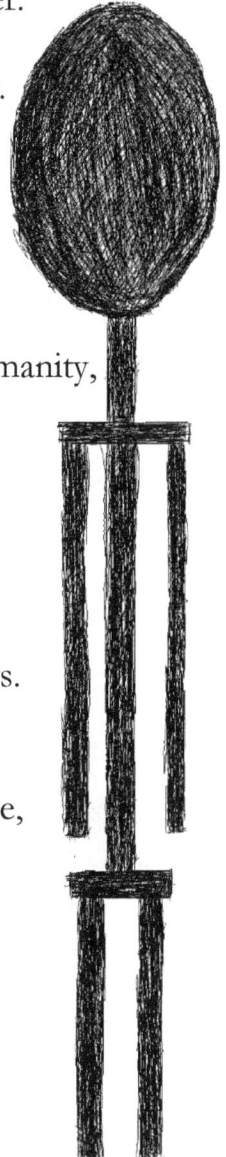

Humanity. Humanity. Confused humanity.
Our recent place in nature is a delusion.
We're suffering from denial and confusion,
Finding ourselves as an imagined top dog,
A top dog, a predator, whose importance is small.
Those at the top are always the most dependent of all.
There's a foundation of life that has given us a chance,
A working food chain from grasses to ants.
We could toot our own horn
If we were as worthy as plants.
Without our green friends there are no humans,
But without humans the world gets better.
Remember that one down to the letter.
It's important to know our scale of importance,
And vital to know how we have it distorted.

Humanity. Humanity. Wake up, humanity.
Before modern humanity, nothing needed preserved,
Not oceans, nor forests, not trees, nor rivers,
Not plants or animals.
They weren't endangered.
Without us, predators and prey
Were in balance in nature.
Wake up, humanity!
We're destroying the only planet we inhabit.
We're gross to the environment like carbon maggots,
Starving for pristine wilderness to bring the havoc.
Havoc?
Havoc?
Is that the only way we'll have it?
Humanity. Humanity. Oh, the humanity.

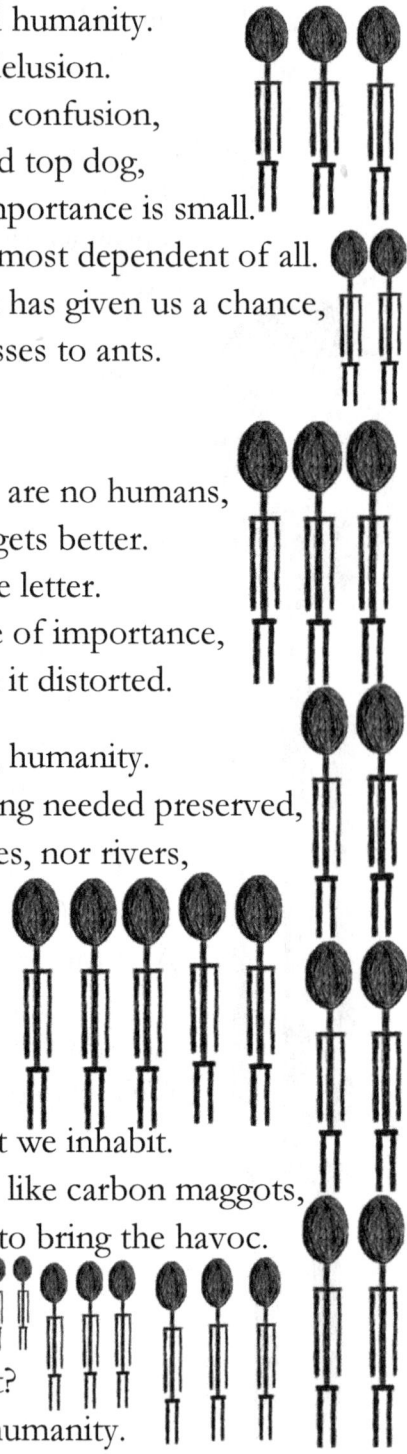

64

Humidity

Humidity. Humidity, Oh, the humidity.
I'm moister than an oyster,
And smothering in a blanket
Of heat and moisture.

I'm freckled and speckled
With polka-dot sweat beads.
I can barely breathe
Among this moisture and heat.

And my shirt's stuck to me
By wet blotches, covering.
It looks embroidered
From this heat and moisture.

Stillness helps none.
The sweat still runs.
I must find some AC
To escape this moisture and heat.

New Resolution

Boring, boring.
Now the weekends are ongoing.
Gone are the ones that were fast and fun
Replaced by days that drag on and on.
Slower than snails, speeding like sloths,
Exciting as soup made of all broth.
Not a second slips by unrealized.
When there's no fun, time doesn't fly.
Stinking New Year's resolution
Might not be the solution.
My willpower is sinking.
Think I'll start drinking.

Gold Digger

Bed, bath, and be gone, gold digger.
I just turned the key on my bank account
And locked you out.
Weaning you off my piggy bank's nipple
Was oh so simple.
Had to do it before my money ran out.
Now I'm on the offense,
Tackling the plans of little princess
On a money quest
Who insisted on a superficial love disguise.
Working me with those eyes and thighs.
Same potion used on other guys.
Fools with a beating heart
Who fell for an actress from the start.
You were playing a role, stealing the show,
Then pretending took its toll.
A little time unwound you.
And soon I found you losing touch.
Handling that greed was just too much.
Now it's over. You've blown your cover.
But don't worry, girl. Just strut your stuff.
Another sucker will fall like a nut.
He'll be a squirrel for your butt.
You'll have his credit card before long,
And be singing the same old song.
Don't look to me for what went wrong.
Away, is where you're going,
Now be gone.

Far-Out World

The far-out world inside my head
Is unbelievably unlimited.
Inside, I could have a chat with you,
Or invite some clones and have a chat with two.

Two of you in front of me,
Oh, it's so easy for me to see.
I'll make three and four, five and six.
They're not that hard, these mental tricks.

My mind's a garden fertile with possibilities
Where, with a seed, I can plant a money tree.
Watch it grow right in front of me,
Then pick and share each and every leaf

With my friends who love to explore
Distant worlds where there's no war,
Where peace comes first on every shore,
Where love matters more and more.

Where, with sleek wings we can fly,
Straight into space, above the sky.
Flying together side by side,
Where gravity's easily defied.

I really want to share these things,
These worlds, and trees, and these beings.
They're so fantastic, you should see,
But that's a wish that cannot be.

Ebb and Flow

Ebb and flow,
A little bit this way,
A little bit goes.
A little bit that way,
A little bit stays.
Life rides the waves,
Of balance to and fro.
It goes without saying,
That we'll always be going.
Changing for change's sake.
Facing the changes made.
Growing and aging.
Ebbing and flowing.

Pickin'

I pick my nose when no one's lookin'.
The guilty party has just spoken.
I send fingers north for digging and hookin'.
Not sure why I pursue these tokens.

Nothing good ever comes from the prying,
And why does the pickin' increase when I'm driving,
And why do I always give them a good eyeing,
And why are they so prolific and thriving?

These buried treasures come in all sizes,
And textures like crusty, dry, sticky, and slimy.
By treasure, I don't mean gleaming gifts or fancy prizes.
I mean foul happenstance from a habit so grimy.

The right tool for most jobs might be the pinky,
And if that doesn't work there's the pointer and ring.
The middle's too big if they're buried too deeply,
But the sticky ones will stick to most anything.

It's hardest to hide when I dig with my thumb.
Getting caught is certainly no fun.
In no situation could I look so dumb.
Even if I was only removing just one.

You can't explain away a finger tipped with a nose seed.
Might as well accept it and hope for sympathy.
Alas, I offer a reason for pickin', a simple need.
When I mine all the boogers, the better I breathe.

Elusive

You ain't kidding the talent is missing.
Stop, look around, and listen.
When's the last time you heard a new song
Longer than three minutes?
Pumping them out for money,
Is the current condition.
Love for the art has been lost with the vision.
Digitized vocals, effort's in remission.
Flashing lights and fancy effects,
Helping no-talents with their hits.
Where's the songs we miss
Composed with strong lyrics?
Who's current and making good music?
If they're out there, they're elusive.
Guess I'll crank up the old tunes,
'Cause they don't make 'em like they used to.

Fine Dying

Fine dining from the finality of dying.
The finest meal has a shadow of a life lost.
For the party eating, there's pleasure,
But there's a party that paid all.
With fork and knife, slice and bite,
But remember to appreciate,
The terrified animal that gave its life.

Gibberish

Thinking of forty-three thrift.
A key broom around it fits.
Head time high low big lift.
Bugs yummy pogo been swift.
Words coming out with a twist.

Pack a seven seen more itch.
Cup tag or bucket lick a ditch.
Low bang loose woody pitch.
My corn horned go rack rich.
Talking, talking with a glit, glitch.

Buy flavor sticks old liver fish.
Nine tally turkeys do feet a wish.
Tie sparks too tight on a dish.
Why lung kick no chocolate swish.
My favorite word is gibberish.

Robotic

Eyes glaze,
Emotional daze,
Lurching muscles,
Mechanical hustle,
Semi-fast,
Boring task,
Repetitive motion,
Brainwash potion,
From the factory
That's after me.

Write Now

Napkin neurosis.
Brainstorming seconds after the strike of idea lightning.
Grey matter quickly sifts out the grey areas,
The details that own no gravity, no importance,
The inventor focuses more on the sort of details
That will further the light and the life of this revelation
In the present tense—the right now.
Turning impulse to concrete,
An invisible thought to a path to tread
That's born of the power of the mind,
The inventor takes action,
Leaping a step ahead and begs a pen
From a passing waitress, hastily.
Making all effort to save the memory
While it floats, slowly sinking,
In a raging sea of distracted consciousness,
With waves crashing and carrying away attention.
The waves dare to disrupt thought.
Fighting the possibility of the idea going under,
The inventor notices and ignores,
One final shout of thunder,
Commandeers a napkin,
And introduces paper to pen.

Formal Introduction

Notice the back of your hand.
Bring your senses to attention.
Notice the shadows highlighting ridges.
Those ridges are wrinkles, marks of your age,
Accompanied under your skin by wiggly veins
That crisscross across the back of your hand.
Now turn your palm to your face.
Send your hand a command.
Move your thumb.
It's large and independent.
Unlike the pinky
That bends another when you bend it.
Your palm has ridges too, but lacks hair.
Spin your hand around,
And notice all the hair back there.
I'll bet if you stare you'll find more hair
Than you originally thought there.
Now grab something.
How about your other hand?
Introduce them to one another,
And imagine the introduction as formal.
Interlock your fingers, the feeling is normal.
This is a meeting of respect and long overdue.
It's time to realize each one is its
Sister or brother, its partner and friend,
Always ready to help; there 'til the end.

I've Seen

I've explored the Himalayas of Colorado,
And I've trekked the Cascades of Kansas.
And I survived the stalking tyrannosaurs
Of both of those ranges.

Without knowing a thing was wrong,
I've opened great concerts with a song
And watched as my audience
Watched me sing wearing nothing at all.

Once, I found the secret to human flight
Lying plainly in the runner's stride.
Faster and faster I ran, steps widening
Until I was no longer landing. I was flying!

And I've also been trapped in slow motion,
Running from an angry mob and its weapons,
Terrified and unable to escape their pursuit,
Until disappearing at the last second.

I've seen whales swimming in backyard pools,
Pools of liquid gold pulled by smiling mules,
Pulled with eagle hair from square spools,
Spun by unruly ghouls from Liverpool.

The most interesting side of me
Lies within each one of these memories.
These wonderful things I've seen,
They all came in a dream.

Another Night's Rest

Grandma, you've passed on,
But we've met once more.
Death is not the authority of our crossings.
For life lives on in memories.
But what's more,
This meeting was no memory.
Our conversation was new.
I spoke to you, and you replied.
You'll be with me until the day I die.
Wonderful dreams obey no harness.
For that, we are blessed.
Grandma, I can't wait to see you again
In another night's rest.

Biological Clock

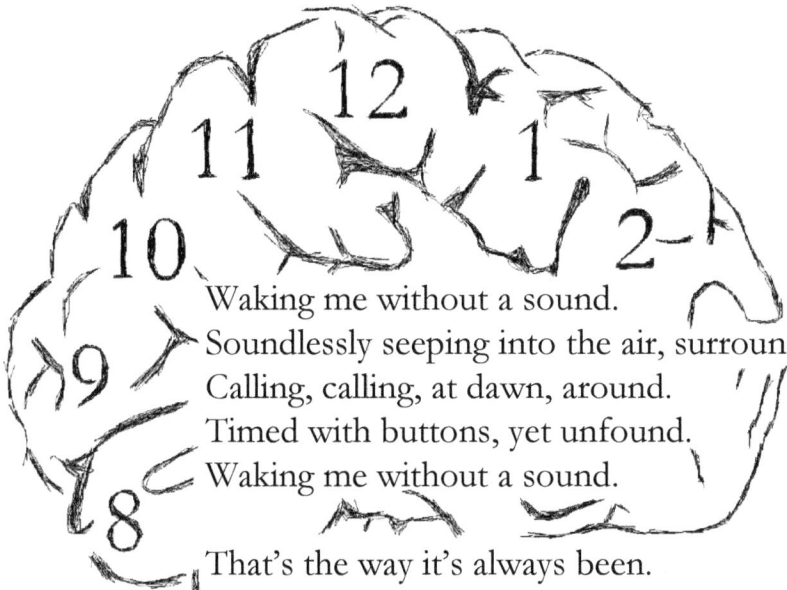

Waking me without a sound.
Soundlessly seeping into the air, surround.
Calling, calling, at dawn, around.
Timed with buttons, yet unfound.
Waking me without a sound.

That's the way it's always been.
Working little midweek then,
Working flawless all weekend.
Monday comes, it leaves again,
Arriving when Friday ends.

Saturday morning alarming soft.
Sunday morning wake-up call.
Ticking, ticking, without pause.
Flawlessly working silent calls.
A biological trick I can't turn off.

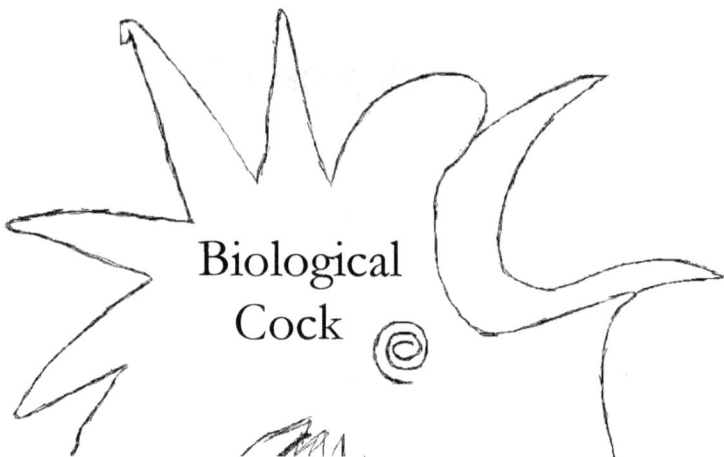

Biological Cock

Waking me with lots of sound.
Blasting into the air, surround.
Crowing, crowing at dawn, around.
Timed with buttons, yet unfound
If it crows again, I'll kill it now.

That's the way he's always been
Crowing, crowing, crowing, then
Crowing, crowing, crowing, then
Crowing, crowing, all weekend
Like he'll never crow again.

Saturday morning, sounding off.
Sunday morning wake-up calls.
Crowing, crowing, without pause.
Back to sleep, I can't fall.
This chicken's really pissing me off.

Biological Prong

Waking me without a sound.
Silently prodding into the air, surround.
Growing, growing at dawn around.
Wow, it's gained half a pound
But if I don't go pee, it won't go down.

That's the way it's always been.
Rising with the sun and then
It's time to drain my little friend.
Relieve him of the pressure when
My bladder's tippy-topped again.

Saturday morning, it's not soft.
Sunday morning, still standing tall.
Answering morning's call of the prong,
To the toilet, I'll strut along
To make a yellow waterfall.

Third Slice

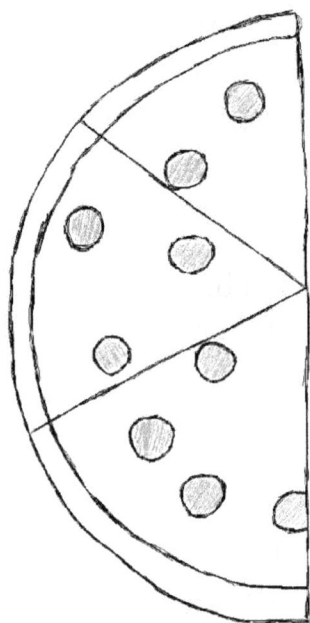

When I'm with you,
I'm in a dream.
Especially when
You're supreme.

Swinging Free

Walking around town
With my zipper down,
I sure do feel the wind.
There's a breeze above my knees,
And a gust below my guts,
And a wind upon my things
That rhyme with butts and guts.
Guts don't rhyme with grins,
But grins are what I'm getting
From friends who see me swinging
So freely in the wind.

Dense

I once described my friend as dense.
By this, I surely meant no offense.
To me, this word worked for my friend,
But it nearly caused our friendship to end.

I was merely trying to describe his mass.
He wasn't skinny, and quite far from fat,
Wide at the shoulder, strong at the back,
How do you describe features like that?

I searched for words but none popped out.
I thought he'd sound short if I called him stout.
But five-ten isn't short, no way, no how.
I thought I'd nailed it without a doubt.

But my friend's as quick as a whip.
He busted me as soon as dense left my lips.
To this day, he will not forget,
And I'm reminded of dense every chance he gets.

Turns out, it was me who was dense.
I'd forgotten the word's other sense,
But now I've found a word that just might fit.
I think my friend looks like he's thick.

You Following?

Hands emoji,
Oil emoji,
Back emoji,
What's it mean?

Hands emoji,
Oil emoji,
Sigh emoji,
What's it mean?

Hands emoji,
Oil emoji,
Hot emoji,
What's it mean?

Hands emoji,
You following?
This emoji collage,
Is a text massage.

The Spider

Six by six by six,
Crawling through the grass and sticks.
Toward some point, you're transfixed.
Flying is one of your wonderful tricks.

And eight by eight by eight,
When we meet, you'll meet your fate.
Away in a corner I shall wait,
For our coming dinner date.

Along you move towards my web.
Thoughts of me, you've all but shed.
I can't wait to see your head,
Looking toward my comfy web.

As you near, you take flight.
Look at you so free and light.
You veer hard to the right,
But you'll not avoid my web tonight.

Your arrival is a welcome treat.
I was in need of something to eat.
I'm grateful you've found a seat
At my web and at my feet.

Now it's time to face my wrath.
It's not personal, just my path.
There's no rescue on your behalf.
There'll be no pain in the aftermath.

Panic grows from deep within.
You twitch and struggle, and I move in.
What must be done, will now begin.
I take hold, and sink fangs in.

Take my venom. Take my cider.
You'd not be here if you weren't a glider.
You found my web the perfect divider,
From your freedom. I'm the spider.

The Recipe

The recipe for a legendary song,
Differs from an ordinary one.
And any creation is unworthy without soul.
So give your song soul straight from a long time ago.
Let it burn. Let fires of longing burn.
Let them burn so long that the long lost return.
Make them hunger for home,
And hang on to the words.
Offer thoughts as sweet as a childhood discovery.
Deliver a melody worth remembering,
A melody that will steal a whistle right from your lips,
And a feel-good, contagious sensation,
That will start you tapping your toes,
Without even knowing.
Endow lyrics with passion and spirit
As meaningful and peaceful as a long-range view
Of a wide horizon and a sea of blue sky
Where the clouds are ships sailing by.
Settle with your lyrics when you love them
Like that pretty girl you'd love to settle with.
Then rest and revisit your music.
When your head is clear and your smile proves
That you've captured magic,
That you've painted the force of life into your work,
You'll have surpassed ordinary.

The Letter

Dear Michael,

Screw your motorcycle. You'll not be riding today.
Last night you stayed up too late. And drank.
And you were an asshole. And you know I'd rather not,
but you insisted I apply the pain through every shot you
drained. I was hoping to fly away, and give a different
drunk a shitty day, but you invited me to stay when
you went and tapped the keg. Then you exclaimed
without regard, "I'll have no hangover tomorrow!
I feel fucking great!" Then you started dancing
with a drunken gal named Nancy, with the grace
of hippos prancing. You were so proud and celebrating.
Down and down the drinks were draining.
Then at three, there was no evading what I had to do,
on which I was waiting. I had to make you pay.
Sorry, Michael, it just works that way.

Sincerely (barely),
The Hangover Fairy

Craziest Thing

I can do this thing,
Where I do this thing,
That will have you saying,
"How can you do that thing
That's got me saying,
That's the craziest thing
I've ever seen.
It's driving me insane.
What does it mean
When you do that thing?"
What do you mean,
What does it mean?
It's plain to see.
It's simply the craziest thing
You've ever seen.

Old Truck

My old truck stopped giving a hoot.
I was late to work, and it wouldn't move.

I cranked it, pushed it, and pulled it around.
A hiccup of smoke, and barely a sound.

There ain't no fun in being broke down.
What am I going to do with it now

That its hauling days have come and gone?
I could park it on the lawn,

And watch it die in a rusty nap,
Plant some flowers in the back,

Or sell it off as a heap of scrap.
It's always been a piece of crap.

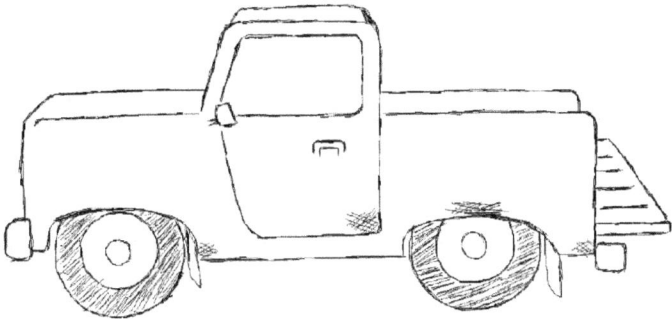

West Virginia

Take your time, West Virginia.
Please, take your time.
When interstates plant repetitive seeds of commerce
Throughout our country,
Shade those seeds with your beautiful trees.
Slow their germination.

Looking like the rest,
Leaves an empty nest of memories.
Let the time of others fly.
Keep yours in a better quality of life.
Let yours know the wild, the mountains, the green.
Let us not be known for concrete.

But show our neighbors our hospitality,
And give them a break from the city.
Invite them in for four-season fun
And autumn's festival of colors,
Its galaxy of leaves starbursting in October.

Welcome them with a ridgeline chorus,
Sung by wind and wildlife.
Let others feel the freedom here,
That we know year round,
But steer them home safely on your twisting roads.

Stay humble, West Virginia.
We don't need to shout
From our emerald mountaintops
That we have the country's oldest river,
Oddly named the New,
And how that river gouged a gorge
That birthed a bridge,
Once the largest single arch in the world.

Don't worry about another record anytime soon.
Authenticity is built with bricks of character,
And is found in being first.
When it's gone, we'll want it back.
Please take your time, West Virginia.
That's all I ask.

No-Good Nothings

The junk in the cellar,
Isn't it depressed,
Living in a darkened, cluttered mess?
Soulless this and thats
Once gazed upon affectionately
Now gazed upon occasionally.
There's a fur coat and knickknacks,
Toys and dishes and old hats.
There are boots and books
And other belongings,
Fillers of other nooks
Worth no merit nor nostalgia.
They're no-good nothings
No longer worth a look.

BS

He said we'll sober up at the bar.
Then he'll drive us home in the car.
But we'll not sober up at the bar,
Or anywhere, near or far from a bar.
We'll not be sober at the bar.
I laughed at his remark.
No one's ever sobered up enough
At the bar to drive a car.

So Good

She looked at me,
And she looked so good.
When she looked at me
I said, "Yes, I would."

Right before
My very eyes
My keys are gone
To no surprise.

Octokeys

Where they went,
It beats me.
I'm fooled again
By my keys.

A metal ring
With metal legs,
It has a brain,
My keychain.

Camouflaging
And vision-dodging,
It's a techno-nature
Metal creature.

Must've moved
On its own
Creeping 'round
My quiet home.

Appearing only
When I'm late.
Spotted hiding
Near a plate.

Soured Flowers

Roses are red
Violets are blue
That's their gang colors.
And you're not in their crew.

The roses are shady.
They've become bad seeds.
It's been that way since
Hanging with weeds.

The violets are hoes.
And the roses are pimps,
Who wear gold bracelets
And grow with a limp.

There are roses on crack
And violets on meth.
What the daisies are on,
Is anyone's guess.

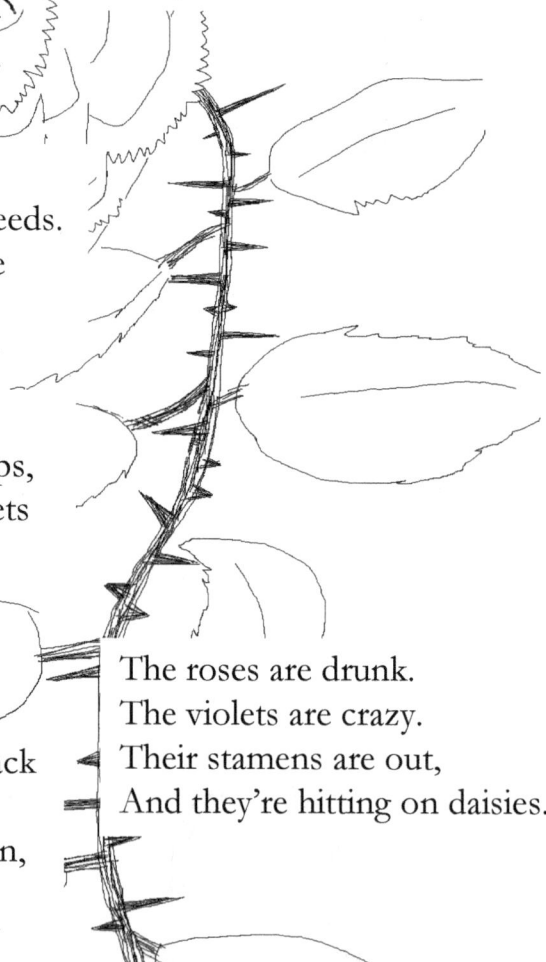

The roses are drunk.
The violets are crazy.
Their stamens are out,
And they're hitting on daisies.

Now the roses have bones
And the violets have teeth.
Since taking those drugs
They've turned into meat.

Hairdoo

I'm not the smartest artist,
Or the sharpest pencil,
But, oh my, I can fart a whistle,
And my poo has bristles
That I can use to comb my hair with.
And that's what a hairdoo is.
And hairdoos are gross.

The Dog and Me

He goes from zero to happy in three point five.
I go from zero to happy. . .
Or do I? Ever?

He stands for what he stands for and never changes.
I stand for change.
Or do I? And why?

He marks, protects, and defends his territory.
If I don't pay taxes, I don't have territory,
And I call the police for protection.

He's strong and fast and agile,
And has bright white teeth he's never brushed.
I'm fat, slow, and my teeth are yellow.
That's fair?

He'll pee anywhere he pleases and does not care.
I can't pee if I get the slightest stare.
What's wrong there?

His world reaches to the store and back,
And he's fine with that.
My world is limited by work and debt.
And I've got it better than my pet?

Natural Love

Love can't be forced unless you're in prison,
But that's just a joke where my point is missing,
So forget about that and have a listen.
Let us imagine two people kissing.
From the outside, their shared attention,
Is easily observed as their lips glisten.
Their facial embrace is the very definition,
Of love in the visible, third dimension.

But what you see is not always what you get.
There's another dimension to it yet.
Dig a little deeper and discover regret,
When you find that one's in relationship debt.
One thinks their whole future is set.
The other thinks about the soulmate unmet,
And dreams of the future and this time to forget.
Their relationship surviving, is an unsafe bet.

Only one knows they're growing apart,
And prays for a change and a fresh start,
And prays not to break an innocent heart,
With a plan they've kept long in the dark.
When they reach the end's critical mark,
One will leave in search of the missing part.
Love can't be forced. It must have a spark.

The Youth

Approaching all things bold
With vigor and soul,
Veiled by inexperience,
There's always hope.
Trial and error,
Conquer, build, and grow,
The harder you climb,
The deeper the hole.
Time is the currency.
There's plenty for the toll.
You can't beat being young
When having goals.

A brazen, naval milestone
Of the nose-hair highway.
Thirty-three years,
Now color doesn't obey my way.
A mark of age? Turning page?
What matters what is right?
Brownish-red, reliable spikes
Now share territory with a white.

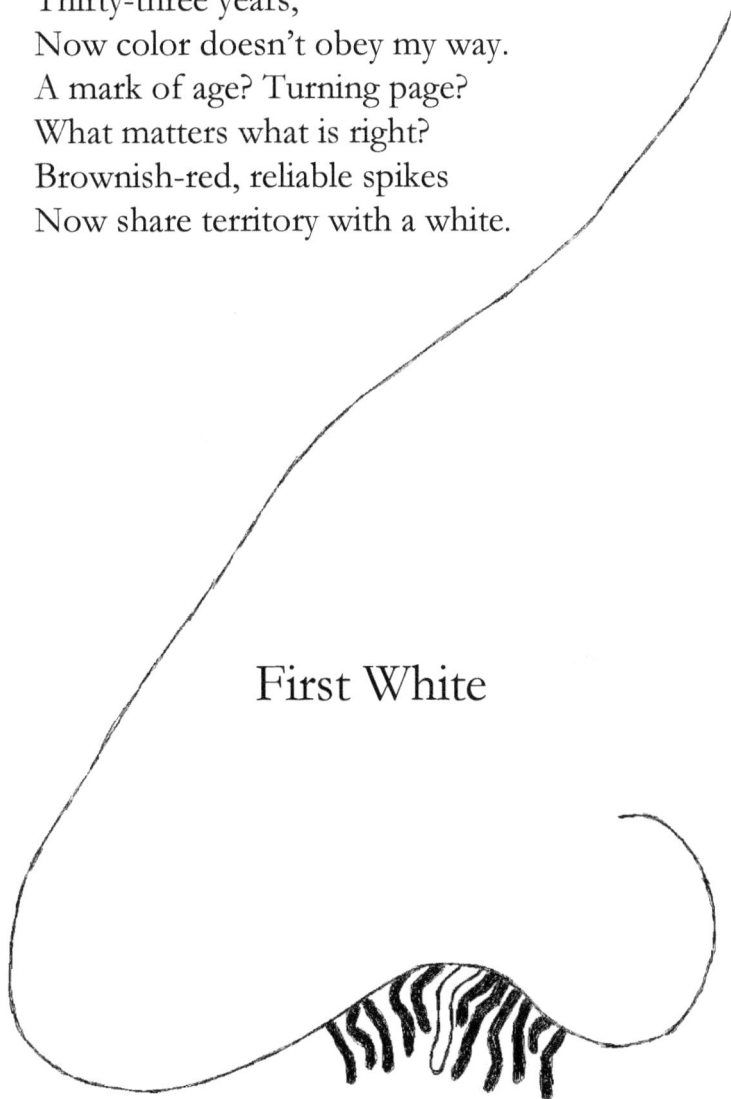

First White

Mexico

I might be able to make it in Mexico.
Might be able to make it a year without snow.
Might be able to make it with a little less dough.
Might be able to make it near a beach,
Still untamed, still wild and free,
In a Pacific wind or Caribbean breeze.
Might be able to make it where I can breathe,
Where there's tradition and humble qualities,
Where family still matters and still gathers,
And where they'd rather not change.
And, oh my, brown-eyed girls never bothered me.
Yes. I might be able to make it in Mexico.

Frogs

Hip-hop minus the hip is all we got.
Let's get that straight from the top.
Ribbit, ribbit, ribbit, and repeat.
Still water sounds so sweet.
Lakes, eggs, tadpoles, legs,
Without fail, we've lost our tail.
Bulging eyes, dining on flies,
Slimy, squishy, ugly prince,
Kiss me first, quickly wince.
Fearless not, fierce not,
We're all about a muddy spot.
And a lily pad,
Yep, those aren't bad.
Pond side pouncing on insect prey.
Praying not to become prey today.
Big wide mouth swallowing whole,
Bullfrog lets out a thundering croak.
Tree frog sends out a little ol' peep,
When the rest of the world is fast asleep.
We're not special. We're not smart.
We're just frogs playing our part.

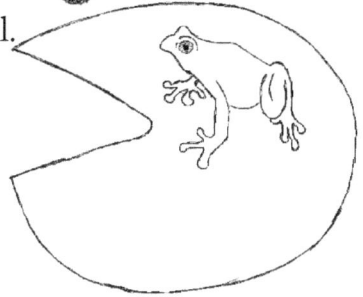

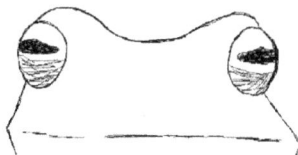

Fourth Slice

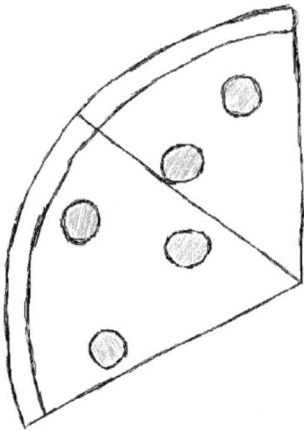

If your life was hard,
I'd make it easy.
'Cause I can't get enough
When you're cheesy.

So Long

We've said goodbye
To the pristine age
With one giant
Carbon-aided wave.
Fast moving
In a technological age,
Earth has seen
Better days.

Bigfoot's Smart

We can't find Bigfoot because he's smart.
Take a big-city big shot for a start.
His trees are buildings and his trails streets.
He knows his way around concrete.
And there are signs that he can read.
He's familiar with all he sees.

Throw an illiterate beast in that scene,
A wild, forest-dwelling being,
Who's never felt asphalt beneath his feet,
Who's never seen a car or penthouse suite,
Who still hunts and kills for meat,
How confusing would that be?

He would be lost from the start,
In a sea of glass and whizzing cars,
Rows of buildings spread out for miles,
The unfamiliar overwhelming his eyes,
Sirens and noise, absence of quite,
Wouldn't he panic in the lack of silence?

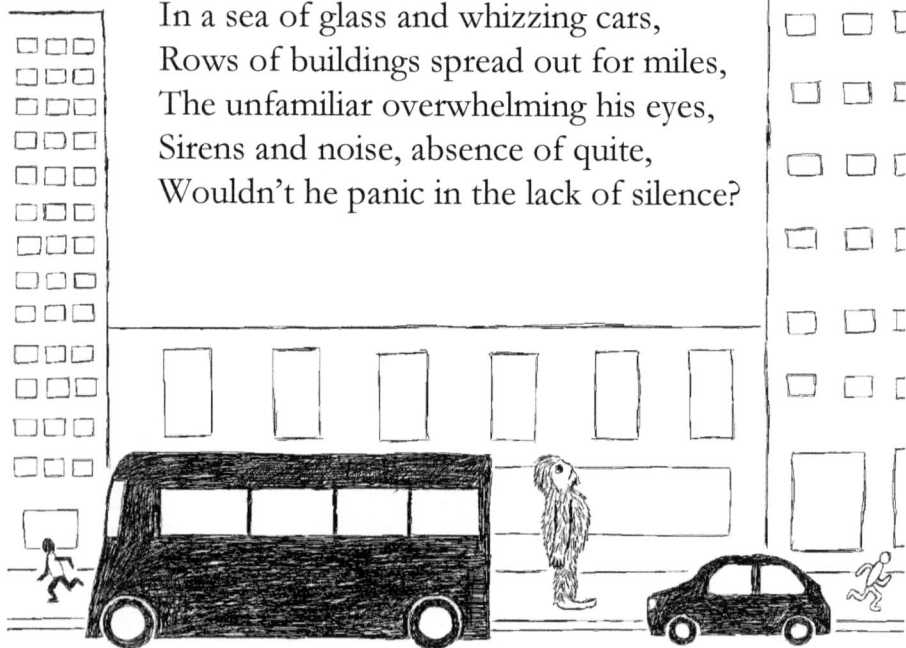

Now put a man in the deep woods,
The stomping grounds of Bigfoot,
A place impenetrable by urban noise,
Where Bigfoot could hear your coming voice.
In the forest, he's the Rolls-Royce.
He'd let you see him, but only by choice.

A man in the woods is as good as blind.
Missions to find Bigfoot are fruitless tries.
The stubborn fail to realize,
Bigfoot's unlike animals of feeble mind.
Out here, Bigfoot's brain is one of a kind.
Hide, nor hair of him, we'll ever find.

He might even be smarter than you and me,
Laughing as we pass by with technology,
Giving ourselves away with lights and beeps,
Cracking twigs, rustling leaves, and whispering.
That's why the mystery's been solved from the start.
Of course, he's real, and he's real smart.

Beer

Here, here, I say.
Here, here, to beer!
Bud has never made me wiser,
But it has made me buddies.
Miller was a few of their names,
And worthy partners in drinking games.
Coors is much the same,
Found in all the stores, that big-brand name.
And that's where it all began,
Drinking from the popular cans.
Consumed in volume, with taste not a concern.
They're beers brewed in a fashion
Where flavor follows the high and price for third.
Then I met Sam. Adams, that is.
Now, there's a flavor I can savor.
Thanks for the beer, neighbor.

My Bud buddies, only like 'em light,
And, to me, that's all right.
Here, it seems like a national right
To drink a beer that ends in light.
But aren't those drinkers sometimes quick to fight?
They don't veer far from their macho-man ways.
They're not like those hipsters who say,
"I only drink IPAs."

And, "Have you had the latest IPA
With that obscure name?"
Wacky Willow, Opossum Litter,
Smackfruit Juice, it's all the same.
Or is it? And that's the thing.

Those are simply names.
From entrepreneurs paving their own way.
Can't blame them for being creative.
Variety is the spice of life,
And some beers are brewed with herbs and spice.
Coriander, ginger, nutmeg, and anise,
Are found in lots of new recipes.
Giving us the widest range of choice
To be enjoyed on a weekend night.
And there's more to be found in other brews,
Through the spectrum of ales and lagers too.

Want a meal in a glass? Have a stout,
Black and heavy, fill up fast.
That's how many have done in centuries past.
Admire the stout and its creamy texture,
Coffeelike taste and caramel color.
Watch its head linger longer than any other.
Pour a porter for much the same.
Enjoy a sweeter taste, but don't complain.
Grab another style: amber, blonde, wheat, or brown.
They're all great to have around.
Go ahead and brew a pilsner, a pale, a red, or a white.
Keep it sterile, remember the hops,
And it will come out right.

Your taste buds and desires
Are as original as the brew you brew.
Thank the yeast for creating the alcohol for you.
Now that it's time to relax and have a few,
Be mindful of moderation's role too.

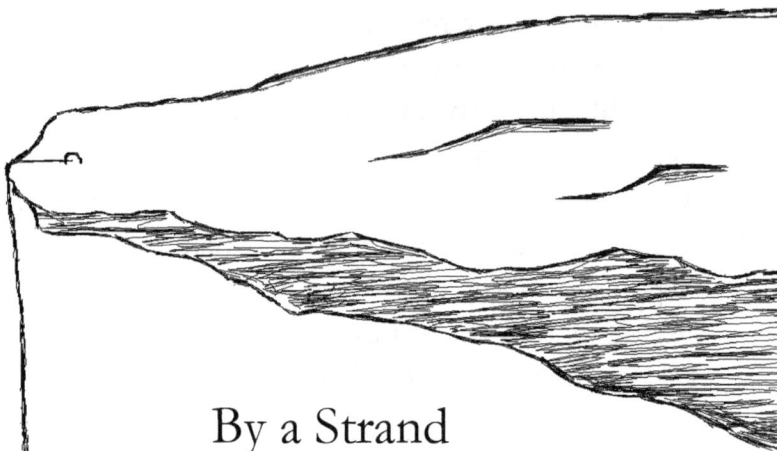

By a Strand

I the climber trust in diameter.
I trust the weight of my bone and tissue
To this product of no living issue.
It must bear the weight of my every memory,
The pain of my family,
The burden of my debt,
Should I fall from this cliff.
Everything that I am,
And every connection I've made,
Hangs from a strand,
Then dangles through my legs.
Thinner than my pinky,
I trust it will hold me.
I trust it will allow a chance
For me to grow into an old me,
And a chance to live fully until then.
And a chance to watch the sun rise and set
Again and again.

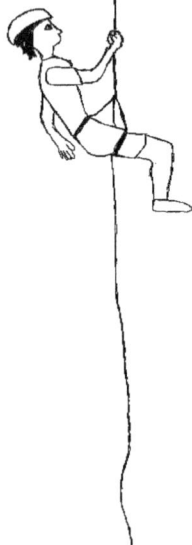

E.A.P.

Edgar Allan Punk,
An unsavory poet who knows it.
Can't fight the urge.
Must pen the dirt.
It won't sell, but what the hell?
When the pen's to paper,
Writing's the savior.

He's a modern-time word mime
Silently trying to define
Ideas metaphorically,
Failing historically,
With words barely rhyming,
Flawed structure and timing.
He mumbles blindly,
Rhymes and little rants.
Words over and over, little chants,
Little chance of catching fire,
In dire need of a dollar,
He's less than blue collar.

He's a starving artist hungry for a hit
And a little green to help a little bit,
To help him climb out of the pit,
The pit he's been digging since forever
Since he can't sense anything better
To do with his time.
For purpose he searches his mind
For a way to get ahead
And again and again
He reaches for a pen.

4 a.m.

It's four in the morning,
The predawn dawn.
There's nothing going on.
She's fast asleep like I want to be,
But my brain is running
Miles in front of me.
Tired signals emit
Then echo through my body,
Like pressure around the eyes,
Repeating and repeating.
This, my mind does not care about.
It simply wants to fight my desire,
And stop my body from sleeping.
Consciously or subconsciously,
Worries manifest and evaporate
Becoming replaced
By thoughts of yesterday.
Then, sometime just before sunrise,
I'll find my peace,
And find myself fast asleep.

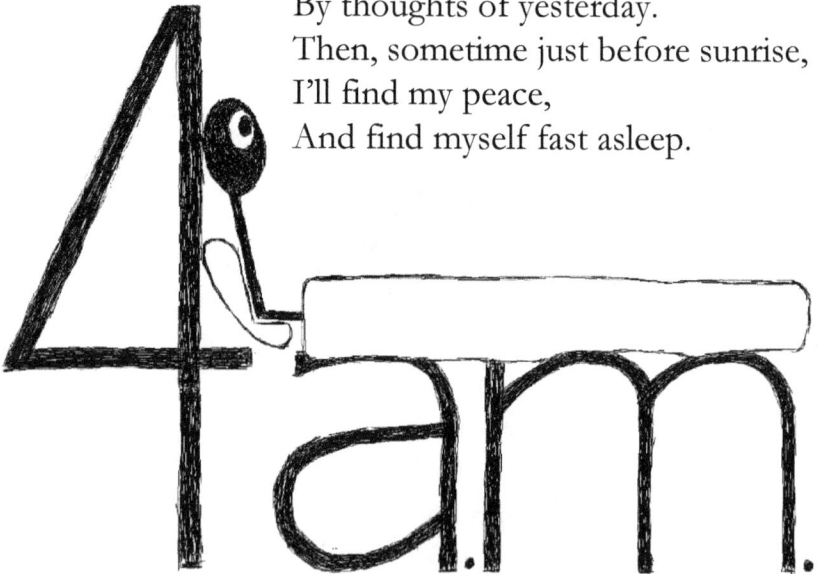

Passionate Passive People

"Awesome!
Let's do it!
Later."

Chickens

I'm a chicken.
I'm a huntin' and a peckin'.
I'm a chicken.
I'm a diggin' and a cluckin'.
I'm a chicken.
Found a bug now I'm eatin'.
I'm a chicken.
Laid an egg by your leg.
I'm a chicken.

I'm a runnin'.
Here comes the ol' farmer.
I'm a runnin'.
He's a lean, mean sucker.
I'm a runnin'.
And he's with the chicken trucker.
I'm a runnin'.
Hauling chickens to their maker.
I'm a runnin'.

I'm a goner.
Farmer's hands 'round my neck.
I'm a goner.
I'm off to get slaughtered.
I'm a goner.
They're killin' chickens against their wishes.
I'm a goner.
Now I'm runnin' around headless.
I'm a goner.

I'm a nugget.
Part battered, part fried,
I'm a nugget.
In a box, as a side,
I'm a nugget.
Take a bite, have a try.
I'm a nugget.

In One Ear

In one ear and out the other.
Son, why don't you listen to your mother?
Be a wise man like your brother.
He's put in the time. Now he's covered.
If you'd just get a job, you'd discover,
Pride in your work unlike any other.

You were the gleam in the eyes of your father.
He saw you becoming a gentleman and scholar,
He believed in your integrity and honor.
He boasted how you would be a doctor,
Or go on to pilot helicopters.
You had so much promise as his grasshopper.

If he only knew how much I've suffered,
Dealing with the stress you put me under.
He'd not stand for this life you've squandered,
Marked by failures, bruised by blunders.
I still can't believe you'd even ponder
A life so wasted. Makes me wonder.

Maria wants to kill me,
And I don't know why.
Something tells me that
In her cold, dark eyes.

They're as pretty as stars
In a warm night sky,
And as foreign as Mars
To an innocent guy.

I fall, sinking into her
Twinkling black holes.
With each glance she grants,
So goes my soul

To an angel of dark,
A seductress of lips.
Her hips warn the closer I get
The more danger I'm in.

She's cast a spell on me,
And I should be forgetting
About her eyes, unforgiving,
And how they're forbidden,

But I'll beg her for mercy.
I'm going to try.
I want you once, Maria,
Before I must die.

Maria

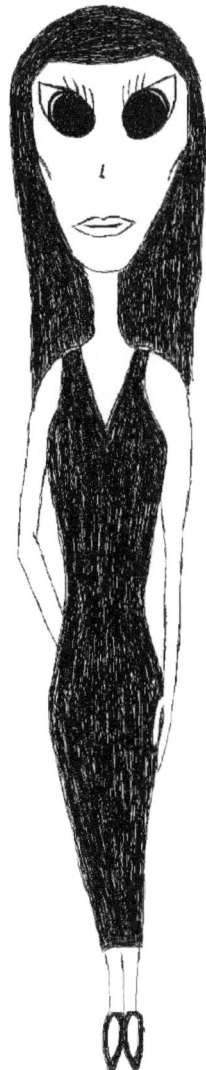

To California

I left for California.
Don't say I didn't warn ya.
That coastal highway's been calling,
And today's that someday.
Baby, I'm on my way.
I'm ready for a redwood ramble,
A high sierra scramble.
I'll start with gas money and end with a thumb.
Find myself at the beach, in the waves, and the sun.
I'm tired of thawing out,
And 'round the corner's spring,
But this year, I promise, it wouldn't change a thing.
I've made up my mind to leave it all behind.
I wanna be humbled by Death Valley.
I want my spirit to rumble in a quake,
To be awakened,
To feel alive.
I can't take it anymore.
It's real this time.
I wanna be excited by the lights of Los Angeles
In the energetic night.
And I wanna stay until I've lost sight
Of what life used to be like.
Baby, I left for California,
To know California,
The whole California,
To find true love in California,
To rise above in California.
Baby, I left for California.
Don't say I didn't warn ya.

Frightful

Oh, the weather outside
Is frightful.
Especially for the guy
On the motorcycle.

Faith

Only trust someone who has faith in you
When their ass is on the line too.
Consequences shared in pairs are far and few.
Don't lose sight of this point of view.
Weed out the junk, and in lieu,
Take the advice and give it a chew.
Work it over for a week or two.
Let it simmer before calling it stew.
Remember, only few truly know you,
And are who you can count on to be truly true.
They're there to guide you through.
Reliable and caring, right on cue.
Be wary of what is brand new
From those not invested in you.
Imagine, for you, a window I drew.
Take a step toward it. Have a view.
If asked where their advice went to.
That should be where their advice flew.
Those who face no consequence, don't have a clue,
And their faith is as good as a handful of poo.

Take A Stand

I don't plan
To leave where I stand.
Instead, an apology I'll demand
From one of my hands.
I can't take this pain anymore.
One hand shut the other's
Finger in the door.

The Rescue

Copper shines bright in my eye.
On a dirty street, I look down and spy
A flat man lying on his side.
Side profile of a famous guy.
I can't just pass him by,
So I reach down and pry,
And respectfully say,
"I got you, Abe."

Free Wanderer

Caged human in a brick-and-stick fish tank,
I'm the homeless wanderer
Passing by at night,
Observing you in soft light
Through glass retaining no water.
I see your television glowing, you unknowing,
Reclining and declining more from life,
Stuck in place, entertained and
Illuminated by a screen advertising
A need for things you don't need.
Fish in fishbowls are more free
Than you in front of that TV.
Out here, walking alone on this darkened road,
I'm as free as a fish swimming the sea.
My wish for you is to someday be as free as me.

The Most

At the end of any spectrum lies a person of magnitude,
An outlier in the population who's the absolute
Happiest, luckiest, holiest,
Oldest, the coldest, the boldest,
Until the boldest meets his demise,
Replaced by the second boldest in line,
The youngest, even if by a millisecond,
The most skeptical, of which questioning beckons,
The ugliest, prettiest, the smallest, and largest,
The sharpest, the quickest, and smartest,
Until the one in number two learns something new.
There's the tallest and fastest, wealthiest and poorest,
The baddest of all time is ol' Chuck Norris.
Some are currently holding Guinness records.
Some will own the worst criminal record.
Whether at the bottom or top of any list
There lies a person at the very edge
Simply defying the averages.

Nosy Neighbor

Business sniffer.
In need of a mouth zipper.

Eyes fixed beyond your front door,
Worried about your neighbor's chores.

Picking up snippets of privacy
Through unwanted, invasive piracy.

Reaching for clues until you got it.
Or make it up through gossip.

One way or another,
You'll invade the other.

Their right to freedom and peace
Is a right you won't release.

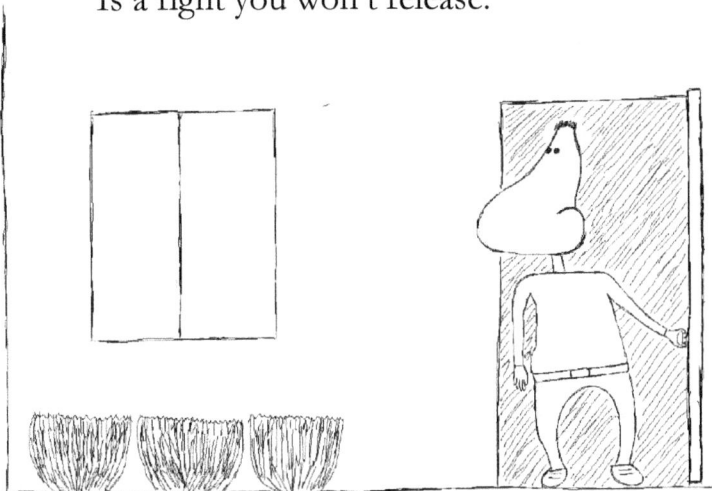

Know a Little

Everyone knows something you don't.
Even if you have the highest IQ,
The densest dunce
Knows something unknown by you.
A matter of intellect,
He'll not come through.
But you have not walked in his shoes,
And cannot know who he knows most intimately,
And what their favorite sandwich might be.
Even if trivial, it is something,
A tiny bit of knowledge
To another human being.
If that makes the dunce happy,
Well, isn't it great
That high IQs don't,
But happy people do
Make the world a better place.

Fifth Slice

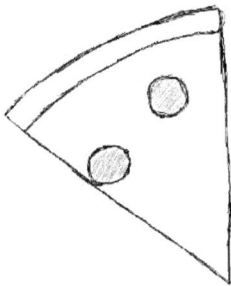

I need to admit
A secret vice.
I'm so addicted
To the slice.

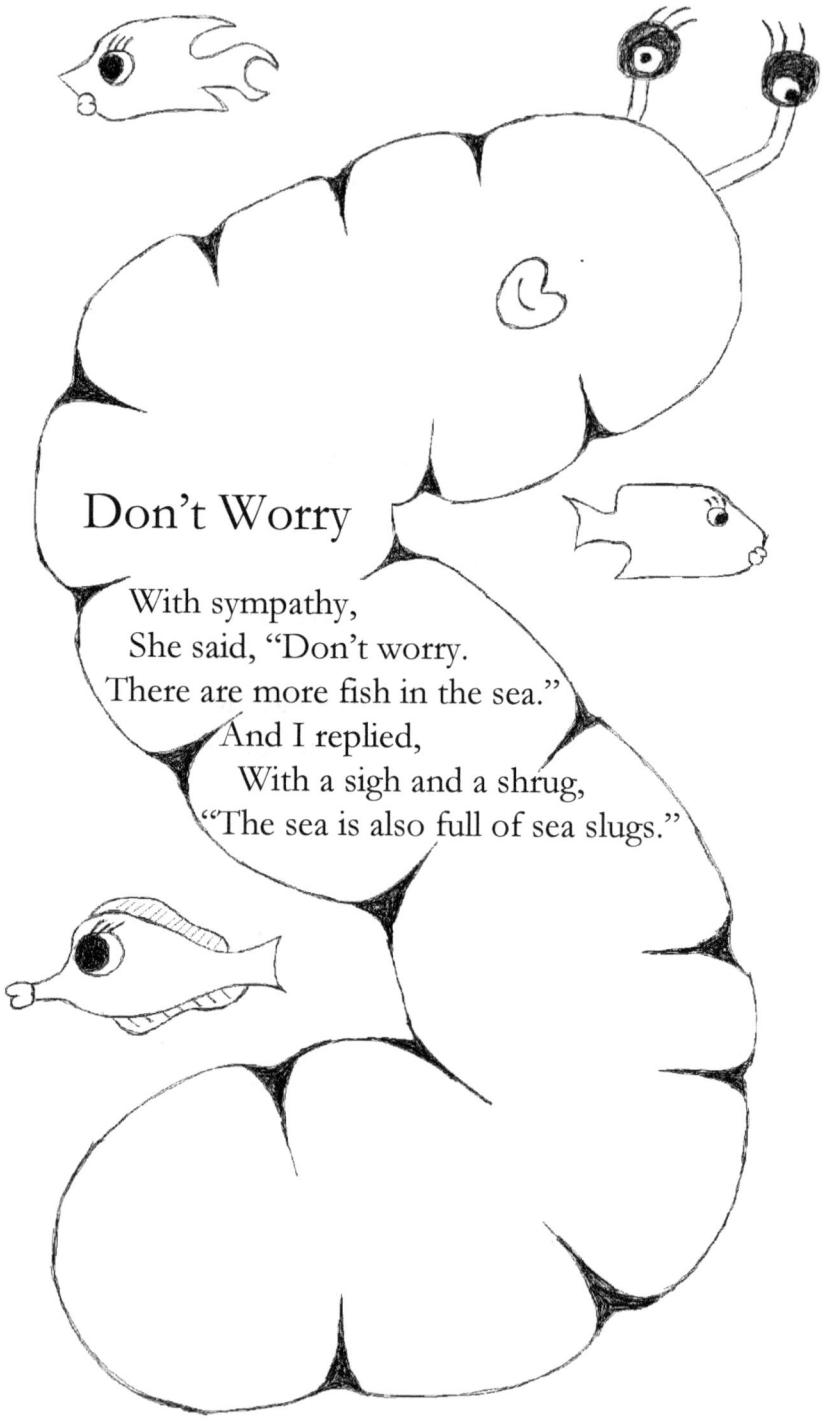

Don't Worry

With sympathy,
She said, "Don't worry.
There are more fish in the sea."
And I replied,
With a sigh and a shrug,
"The sea is also full of sea slugs."

Walking Wherever

Headlights pass me in the night.
Where are they going?
State to state on an interstate?
From a tired state, to a rest stop,
Awake until tired again?
Modern folks can't help but move.
Moving keeps us and our life's ideas alive.
Cold wind, hot sun, dark night out.
Inside their anywhere wagons
Is a careless atmosphere.
Seventy degrees, conditioning,
And entertained along the way.
Nothing slows us anymore.
Traversing distance is easy,
Too easy, so easy,
Think I'll finish this trip in a car.
Where am I going?
Wherever I please.

Cry for the Rhino

Cry for the rhino.
Say goodbye to the rhino.
We're asking them to leave.
We're showing through our actions
How foolish we can be,
We're showing the whole world
Man's selfishness, indeed.
We're driving them away
For ivory monuments of greed.

I'd beg of you to help,
But time has shown,
There's nothing left to do,
But cry for the rhino.
Those of us who care,
And don't want to see them go,
Have failed to overcome
Those who want to poach.
What monsters we've become,
That we do this to the rhino.

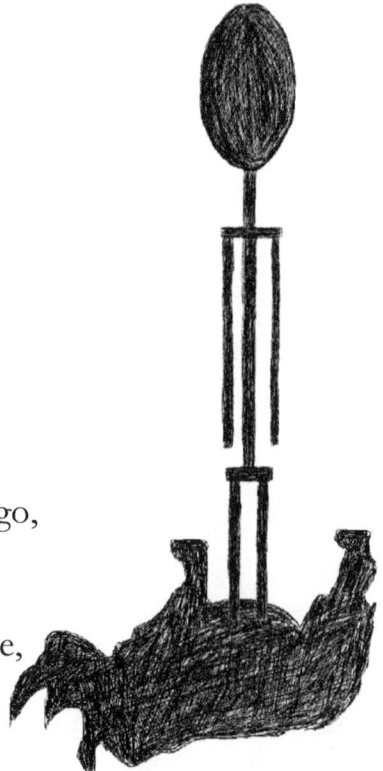

Records will show foolish, foolish man.
So caught up in himself,
He would not share the land.
He lived without regard,
And with his heavy hand,
Continued on his wicked path.
Feed the greedy was his brand.
Extinction is a consequence,
Another side effect of man.

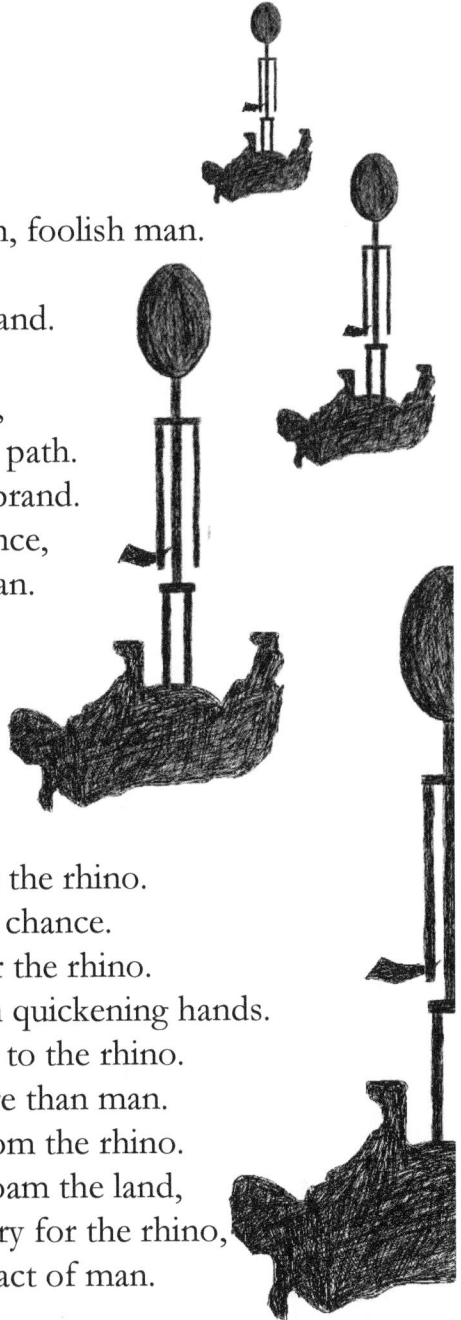

Time is running out for the rhino.
They deserve a fighting chance.
Most won't even try for the rhino.
The clock's ticking with quickening hands.
Prepare to say goodbye to the rhino.
They need a savior more than man.
I hope we learn why from the rhino.
When they no longer roam the land,
I'll hang my head and cry for the rhino,
And never forgive this act of man.

Paradise

Paradise is all in your head.
Such a place can't exist.
The curse of paradise is loneliness.
What sounds perfect to me,
Might not work for Fred.
Fred's got a different scene in his head.
In his paradise, I couldn't exist.
And frankly, Fred's not in the paradise in my head.
I'd be a glitch in his paradise.
He might imagine a cabin in the woods,
Miles from anywhere amongst plentiful wildlife.
A simple existence where life is slow and easy.
Something out of a past century.
That's for Fred,
But not for me.

It only takes one person, one thing,
One time, one undesired being,
For there to be no difference between
Paradise and reality.
My paradise is in my interpretation,
And it starts with a tropical location,
Full of resources, minus the bugs,
A sandy beach, no sweat, no debt,
Cool drinks each night at sunset,
Plenty of time, always seventy-five,
My closest friends and family.
Anyone else, and paradise would be lost.
Others in my fantasy come with a cost,
Like quarrels and uncertainty,
Anxiety, and unwanted choices.
Paradise evaporates in the fog of
Too many voices.

Friday Night

Friday evening at my place.
Pick up the phone. Start the calling.
Fire up the grill. Provide the steaks.
Bachelor pad, perfect space.

Magnetic friends, free fun's drawing.
Music's loud, lots of bass.
Keg's ready for tap installing.
Cars arrive full of friends they're hauling.

One drink down, two down, hurried pace.
Liquid fun, third drink's calling.
Get 'em in like a race.
Faster, faster, forget the taste.

No need to think, no need for stalling.
Drink 'em up by the case.
We've drunk so many, no recalling.
Pounding beers, beverage mauling.

Plaster-faced facing drunken grace,
Falling, slurring, climbing, crawling,
Here, there, all over the place.
Leave a trace with a broken vase.

Unstable feet, risk of falling,
Angry demeanors are embraced.
I hear shouting, here comes the brawling.
As a group, intelligence has fallen.

Now I'm a four a.m. philosophy ace.
An hour of preaching, it's appalling.
Religious views, politics, and race,
Spewing out of my drunken face.

Distracted by my wiener calling,
Neighbor girl, shoot for home base.
Insulted her, now she's bawling,
She is gone, the sun is dawning.

Night's over, no tail to chase.
Climb in bed, shoes on, and sprawling.
Memories are wiped without a trace.
The last few hours were a disgrace.

In an Intersection

We pass one another
In an intersection.
Driving in opposite directions.
Eye contact,
And we're in sync,
Two minds thinking
The exact same thing,
"What are you looking at?"

You're a natural wonder
Who makes us wonder
Why you do what you do
And how it comes
So naturally to you.
Your mind's a wonder too.
It's fine at least half the time,
Until you find a lazy little kitty.
Then some primeval need
Leads you astray
Toward another stray
Without a need for you today.
No. It needs not what you give,
But you give what you got
Until you've caught all the lazy little kitties
In the nearby towns and cities.
You call it love, and you call it help,
But the only help needed is help for yourself.
Your neighbors burn with concerns,
For the kitties that you herd,
Knowing there's no escape
From their one-way stay
With all the other lazy little kitties
Who met the same fate.

Crazy
Cat
Lady

Quarrelling Couple

Piss and moan, gripe and groan,
Frown and scowl, and stop right now.
Not so quick!

Fight and sneer, bite and peer,
Claw and scratch then detach.
But wait a second!

Stomp and cuss, thrash and fuss,
Rage and rip, and get over it.
Yeah, right!

Chase and hit, break and spit,
And throw and awfully nasty fit.
Still not done!

We'll damn and slam and cram and jam,
Each flaw down the other's throat,
Until we,

Crush and mush and discredit the other,
Until there's nothing left,
Then,

Cry and regret, crack and submit,
Kiss and hug, and acknowledge our love.

What a Mess!

Stanley's stomach is rumbling,
Warning of an ultimate act of repulsion.
Inside his tummy, there's grumbling,
A sign of pressured propulsion.

His muscles tighten in his chest and neck.
Saliva flows to the point of dripping.
Like the sweat on his brow, that's now wet,
Something's coming worse than spitting.

Oh no! The herky-jerky dry heaves,
Are attacking his abdomen!
He's covered his mouth with his sleeve,
And he can't believe this is happening.

There's no way to release it with ease.
Holding it back is futile.
It's awful how he believes,
He can internalize the vile.

Here comes the explosion!
Three, two, one—signal distress!
The reaction's in motion!
He projects a mile, no less! What a mess!

Perfect Ten

I look at you, you perfect ten,
And I say, "Life ain't fair."
You have perfect hair,
An angel's face and sensual stare
The perfect legs and perfect pair
And I've noticed,
The perfect derrière.
Your complexion's worthy of a reflection.
You're the definition of female perfection.
Did I mention you live in a mansion?
And your children could be named
Beautiful and Handsome.
I'd kidnap you and want no ransom.
Just five minutes of your attention
Could ease my tension.
Five minutes where you'd smile and listen.
Too bad your taste in men is expensive.
My meager pension is of insignificant interest
Even if you knew my good intentions.
Perfect tens are attracted to men
Whose assets are extensive,
Leaving me pessimistic.
Though I compare,
I guess I shouldn't care.
It's naïve to believe that life's ever fair.

Why?

No, I don't drink no more.
I don't drink on Monday through Sunday.

No, I don't drink no more.
Friday used to be a fun day.

No, I don't drink no more.
I hope to smile again one day.

No, I don't drink no more.
Seems that my friends have gone away?

That's right. I've quit.
I've danced for the last time.

That's right. I've quit.
Never again, will I feel so high.

That's right. I've quit.
Now I'm bored all the time.

That's right. I've quit.
And I don't know why.

Just how picky is too far for picky?
Some won't eat that because it's sticky.
Some won't eat this because it's green.   Picky
Some deny that food, sight unseen.

Some complain, "That smells weird,
But you say it's good.
I'd try it if it smelled better.
I really would."

Others spout, "Oh, not those! I won't eat them.
They look like they're made of phlegm.
But I believe you. I'm sure they're great.
Oysters just don't fit my taste."

Then there's asparagus, brussels sprouts, and broccoli.
"Good God, man, that's not for me.
Those taste like grass and that's for cows.
I always order the same while dining out."

"Give it to me plain as plain can be,
A burger, bun, and a little cheese.
Now, that's good eatin'! Don't you see?
I wish you'd just leave me be."

"Someday I'll explore with confidence,
The varied menu of condiments.
But for now, I'm sticking with what I know,
Ketchup, mustard, relish, and mayo."

"Question for you. Hope you don't mind."
"Sure, I guess I have the time."
"At world's end, when we're fighting for scraps,
Will I still have to hear about this picky crap?"

Germaphobe

Reject nature.
Priority clean.
Never mind a cellphone's germier
Than a toilet seat.
Look it up if you don't believe.
And never mind the germs floating
In the air you breathe.
Try getting rid of them
By spraying them clean.
And never mind the bacteria
In your mouth. It's obscene.
Or the microorganisms
Inhabiting your body.
Only ten percent of your body
Has human DNA.
The rest of you isn't really you, I say.
Ninety percent of what makes you, you,
Are uninvited hitchhikers.
Isn't that scary?
All of those cooties,
Along for the ride.
Your ingredients.
Your insides.

A.D.D.

My A.D.D. won't let me

Hater

Hater, hater,
Personality like a cheese grater,
Abrasive soul, sole decency evader,
Drive away friends like an alligator.
Best advice, get a life.
Get off the wagon of pain and strife.
Strong beings of positivity
Positively won't take you seriously
When making your points forcefully.
Still, your negativity, you'll spread
On a comments section on the Internet,
Or in public from a distance,
A safe place of low resistance.

Hater, life is better
When you watch that mouth.
Take a second before letting it out.
Calm down, no need to shout.
Overreaction is a sign of doubt.
Doubt in yourself, and this we know,
Because we've learned as we've grown
Your mentality is a problem you own.
Life has a funny way of making this shown.
Through reflection, and with age,
Life can adopt a better stage,
But one must learn along the way
Being nice to others will brighten your day.
A last note to you, only one.
The people you fool equals none.
Instead of hating, spend time on fun.
And with you, I am done.

Her Hands

Your warm hands fit mine better than a glove.
They're a part of you that I really love.

Your soft, warm hands are always welcome to touch my skin.
I cherish the way they feel, and that's how it's always been.

The gentle touch of your warm hands makes me feel superb.
I long for their touch. Can't get enough.

The way you use your lovely warm hands inspires me.
I'm full of satisfaction when your warm hands are in action.

And in the times when it's just you and me,
And the lights are low, and the room is dark, that's the best.
You use your hot, hot hands unlike the rest.

Those moments drive me wild with desire.
Yes, your sexy hands make me feel like the manliest man.

I can't say how much your warm hands turn me on.
I can only reflect on their wonderful effect.

But your cold hands, my God, your cold hands!
Keep those damn things away from me!

Note to Self

Note to self,
I'm a screwup.
Been that way
Since I grew up.
That's what people say.
I just don't get it,
This world that we're living in.
I wouldn't be a villain
Had I designed the world
That we're living in.
Instead, I'm living in
A world designed by other men.
A world where peace is ignored,
Where men are in a race war,
And in a race for
Capitalism success.
That's what's best.
Anything less,
And you failed their test.
So, I failed.
I'm a loser
Who's a boozer,
Drinking away the pain,
Alcohol medicating,
Meditating on what mistake
I'll make today.
Maybe later I'll get it.
But can it sink in?
Or am I too gone
To learn their right from wrong?

Closed Minds

Closed minds
Are no better than
Open wounds
When influenced
Upon the youth.

There's Hope

Legends were once
Newborn,
No-named,
Nobodies.

The Powers That Be

The illusion of power is robust among the most dependent.
Without the secret service, how safe is the president?
Without the nameless agents in the big white residence,
I ask, how safe is the president?

The powerful, the wealthy, those with a crown
Foolishly see the world as their playground.
Where nameless drivers drive them around,
Where nameless gardeners manicure their grounds,
Where systems are in place to keep us down,
Where without assistance and assistants,
Their worlds come tumbling down.

The dependent have lost sight of their vulnerability.
The dependent fail to recognize their organic humanity.
My fellow man, I want you to see
That the powers that be are you and me.

For an hour, for a day, for a week or more,
For as long as it takes to crack their core,
We can bring the powerful to their knees
By simply ignoring what they need us to be.

For an hour, for a day, for a week or more,
When we need relief from their corrupt illusion,
We can overcome them by simply refusing.
We can suffocate them with our influence.

For an hour, for a day, for a week or more,
For as long as it takes to crack their core,
We can expose the weak, the most dependent,
The incredibly needy and greedy one percent.

For an hour, for a day, for a week or more
We can stop being the gardener, the maid, the driver,
The chef, the serviceman, the security,
The soldier, the pilot, the contractor
If we find them drunk on their power.

Their power is in the obeyed illusion.
Alone, they can't operate an institution.
Alone, they're nothing more than a solitary human.
Utterly dependent upon the powers that be.
Utterly dependent upon you and me.

Fear no power. Fear no solitary human.
Fear no struggle. Ignore their illusion.
We are the strong. We are the independent.
Without us, without the powers that be,
How safe is the president without you and me?

Soul Movement

Dancing is soul movement seen in the real.
Dancing is a soul out of hiding,
Escaped from the imprisonment of the body.
It's the sight of a mischievous soul
That's abandoned its post,
And is playing with its host.
It's a body relaxed, but not in slumber,
Not under normal function.
A soul finding form
In flowing movement and motion.
A soul acting out a fantasy,
Through the portal of music, rhythm, and lyric.
For a life's split second,
It's possible to view the human spirit.
Though temporary as long as we breath,
And our nature is physical,
The soul can only flirt with freedom.
The music will cease.
The portal will close.
The soul will return to hiding,
Waiting to dance forever,
After its time in the body.

High Heat

High heat is frying my brain.
My honey's cooking,
Is driving me insane.
Year one, I survived,
Burned food, black, and dry.
I'd smile so she'd feel fine,
While using my teeth to keep my tongue,
From speaking my mind.
Bless her heart, she could burn water.

Year two, I made it through,
Plates and plates of scorched food.
What am I going to do,
Without being rude,
To show her that I'd like to chew,
On food that's tasty and tender too?
I don't want to make her blue,
But I'd rather eat an old shoe.

Year three, somebody help me!
My little honey's in dire need,
Of a proper cooking technique.
I don't want to say a thing,
And harm her self-esteem,
Since she's my little queen,
But she only knows one cooking speed,
And spins that knob straight to high heat.

Another weekend night.
Something ain't right.
Headed for trouble.
Another street fight.

Street Fight

No time to bob and weave.
Out the door, goes technique.
Crowd formed 'round wanting to see,
A cold knockout and hail Marys.

Two idiots talking trash.
Egos soaring, about to crash.
One will stand. One will last.
This one will be over fast.

The big guy's sober,
And the little guy's drunk.
The big guy's over it,
And the little guy's drunk.

Little man's bulletproof and ten feet tall.
His chest's puffed out real wide and all.
He can't stop that mouth and he ought,
To take a moment for a second thought.

Provoke, provoke, instigate.
The crowd already knows his fate.
He's in too deep to get out now.
He's never been so damn proud.

Big hard hook, and the little guy's down.
Laid out flat on the ground.
A thundering crack, what a sound!
My, that knockout was profound!

Sixth Slice

Say what you want
About healthy stuff.
As far as pizza,
There's never enough.

Little Wiener

The large man with the pleasant demeanor
Just left smiling with his hands
Gripping his little wiener.
Once a week, he stops by.
Just for a moment, just to say hi.
I look forward to his visits.
He's a hell of a guy.
And I don't mind if he leaves
With his little wiener in hand.
He's good business
For my hot-dog stand.

The Survivor

Fight to the death to save a few steps.
Fight off others with gestures and threats.

Force your bumper upon them as leverage.
Then toss away dignity, and throw a canned beverage.

Punch the gas to pull in as quick as you can.
Let out a hoot and throw up a hand.

Your walk to the store will be the shortest duration.
One spot closer was worth confrontation.

You're a hazard to other drivers,
But you've earned the space. You're a survivor.

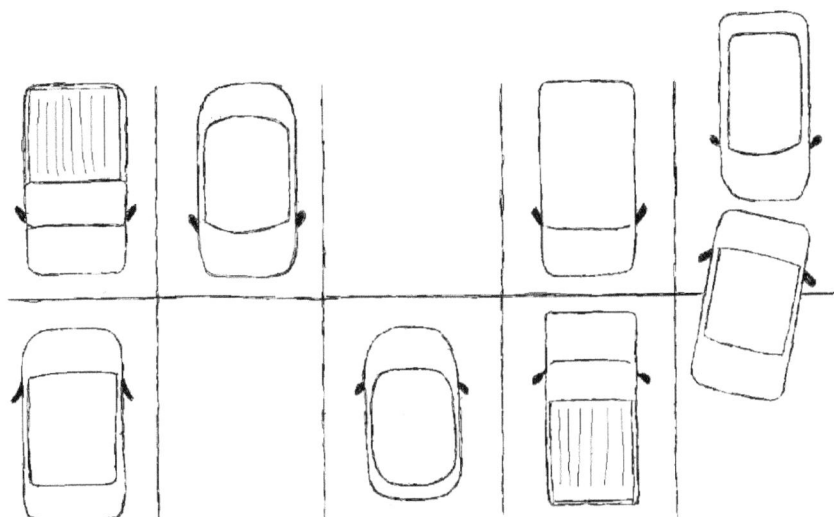

Yankee Doodle

Yankee doodle went to town.
    Or did he?

He stuck a feather in his hat.
    Or did he?

He called it macaroni.
    Or did he?

He met a skeptic,
And it was me.

Pantyhose

The handiest clothes
Are pantyhose.
On a woman,
All stretched out,
Or a burglar's head,
Still stretched out.
Useful beyond any doubt
For hiding something
You don't want out.

Creeper

"What's good, girl?"
"Security's good. Where's the bouncer?
How about you pull up a stool at the bar,
Order another twelve-ouncer,
Drink it quick and order another.
You'll need to be drunk
When you're getting your head thumped."

"Yo, girl. Let me buy you a drink."
"Okay, make it pink with a shot of game.
For you, of course.
Do I have to get the bouncer
To remove you with force?
Take a step back. You're creeping me out.
One inch closer and I'm going to shout."

"Let me get that number, girl."
"Sure. It's 911.
The bouncer's behind you and ready to dial.
Now turn around, apologize, be polite, and smile.
Anything less and he'll punch a hole in your chest.
Then he'll dial that number just like you asked."

"Damn girl! You thick!"
"That may be so, but I'm not thick headed.
And from the looks of it, you better be kidding.
The bouncer's heading your way,
And he's tired of your shit.
He's ready to introduce your face to his fist.
So, good luck with that, Prince Charming.
See you later.
Look for my get-well card,
When you're on that ventilator."

"Sup, girl, whatchu doin' later?"
"I don't know what I'm doing,
But I can see your future.
It looks terrible, and you're nearly toothless.
I'm seeing a vision of you with a foot up your ass,
And it came from that bouncer,
And it happened so fast.
Oh, and there's another vision of you on the floor.
Crying like a baby and crawling for the door."

Working Juan mows one lawn at a time.
Working Juan builds one house at a time.
Working Juan does not commit crime.
Working Juan is good all the time.

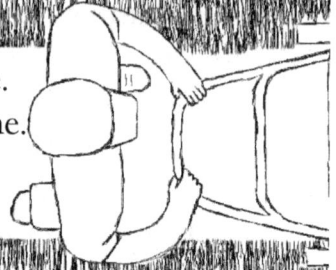

Working Juan

The country he's from is full of corruption,
Where the government contributes little to nothing.
Its power and wealth is poached off of others.
After a while, those citizens feel smothered.

Our country is not immune to the plagues of power,
But it's negated enough not to be sour.
A man can grow here. His children can flower.
His family can prosper if he puts in the hours.

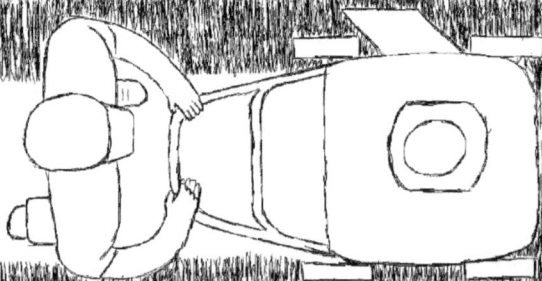

Juan sees America through different eyes.
There is potential here, and he hasn't lost sight.
He risked everything to get here, even his life.
America's a tree that supports those willing to climb.

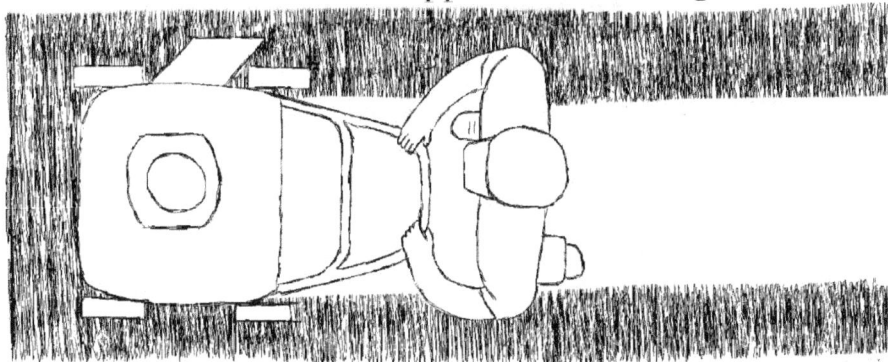

Some who are born here neglect the opportunities.
They're caught in a revolving trap of petty things.
Toward government help, they're submitting.
Nothing could make those citizens more of a pity.

Working Juan is thankful and feels his life is divine.
He will put in the hours and show up on time.
Never complaining, he'll always be fine.
Because he doesn't mind mowing one lawn at time.

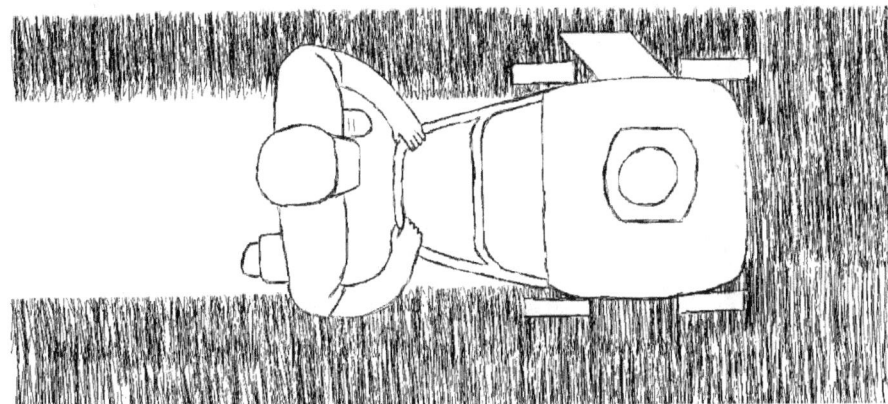

Penguins

What a curse to be born a bird that can't fly.
Should anything provoke more of an animal to cry?
And to inhabit lands of cold and ice.
The short end of the stick,
Penguins own that slice.

They're waddling weirdos of the winged world,
Just shy of being stranger than flying squirrels.
Did penguins deserve wings that evolved into flippers?
Even bats have one up on them,
And they're not birds.

Cross a porpoise and a potato,
And that's what penguins are like.
They can't tell us about their frustration inside.
So, I'll use my voice to express their absence of flight.
I'll climb to a perch way, way, way up high.
Where they can't go, and I'll scream, "WHY!"

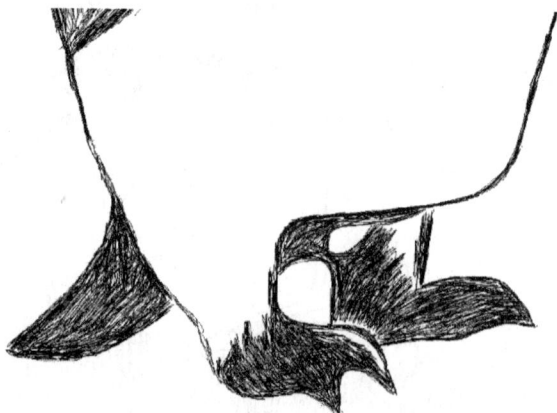

Case Closed

I remember the time you laughed when I stubbed my toe,
The time you forced me to a play when I cared not to go,
The time you made me the brunt of a joke.
I'm saving the anguish for the perfect show.

That April Fool's when you said the house was on fire,
Or that night you guided me into an electric fence wire.
Oh, and the time you volunteered me for the choir.
Paying you back is my highest desire.

That prank call you set up was a barrel of laughs.
Having your ex, the felon, call and threaten my ass.
You got a kick out of me apologizing so fast.
Enjoy it now, because I'll get you back.

When the time is right and you're in the shower,
I'll summon a good one, full of wind and power.
There'll be heat behind it, fermented and sour.
Then I'll unleash the beast I'd been holding an hour.

You'll join me in bed. Revenge will be faced.
You'll lay down your head and get a quick taste,
Of freshly polluted bedroom airspace,
From the fart seeping from your pillowcase.

Positive Thinking

The power of positive thinking
Is greatly enhanced while drinking.
So much so, it's impossible to say no.
Want another beer? Yes!
Want a shot? Why not!
Tequila? You betcha!
Wanna buy a round for the house? Start pouring!
Can you whoop that guy? Absolutely!
Can you do it quickly? Just watch me!
Everything's a go
When drinking takes away "no."

Crotchety Old Man

He'd piss on his fingers then shake your hand,
Then tell a dirty joke as quick as he can,
And laugh as he finds you're not a fan.
To spread his filth, that's his plan.

But that's all the humor you'd get out of him.
He's normally solemn and grim.
His brightest days are cloudy and dim.
Ruffling feathers is fine with him.

If you're in trouble, he's the last to call.
If you kicked the bucket, he'd have a ball.
Toward the world, he's built a wall.
He doesn't want you around at all.

Once I saw him provoke a trip,
Toward a woman with a lame hip.
She collapsed, then his hat he tipped,
And produced a smile upon his lips.

Rotten, wrinkled, mean, and bold,
What in the world has gotten a hold
Of this old man, rigid and cold?
To the devil, it's said, his soul was sold.

So, at his wake, there'll be three,
Sending him away eternally,
A mortician, a preacher, and me.
I'll be there to surely see

That his wretched corpse is dead for real.
His cold skin, my hand will feel.
Then, from my suit, I'll reveal
A jar of piss. His last meal.

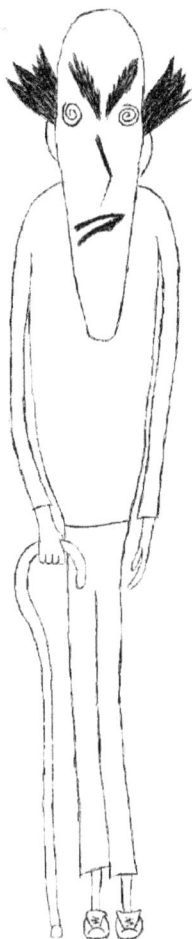

Far From Perfection

All my choices have been tallied,
Equaling a pathetic grand finale.
Less than stellar is where I'm suited.
'Cause let me tell you, I'm flirtin' with stupid.

Everywhere I've gone, I should've gone right,
But I went left, then clean out of sight.
Can't go back now, the past is the past,
However, my path is leading to last fast.

If my breath was measured by my vulgarity,
I know you'd stand a mile away from me,
And, if my habits are any indication,
I'm following a course toward devastation.

My bad choices are noises born of uncertainty.
That's a character flaw I know most perversely.
Uncertainty and me have a relationship of flirting.
We sing to one another through hesitant wording.

I dishonestly use white lies to blind eyes,
To hide obvious feelings inside.
I wear a false persona like a suit of armor.
I'm just an act like a snake charmer.

And there's the part where I'm perpetually perplexed,
As I feebly ponder intellectual text.
That's right, I'm so far from perfection,
I should've succumb to natural selection.

So anymore, I don't even question,
When someone shares a self-improvement suggestion.
I absorb it and run like the wind,
Somewhere for me, there's a finer end.

Betty Rumble

Never was I ever so humbled to stumble,
Upon the old biker babe Betty Rumble.
Part toothless, part ruthless,
Part sassy, part nasty,
Part gross in pantyhose.
Top heavy, if not for her bottom,
Like bad fruit, she was all but rotten.

She desired to be a lover,
But had a way about her
That made her more of a giver.
She delivered more than I desired
On our shared most wild night ever.

Her crooked fingers, gorilla grip,
And hands laced with wormy veins,
Are now inescapably engrained in my brain
From the night she fell in love at first sight,
And I found myself as Betty Rumble's
Midnight delight.

A divey dance hall was host to her courting.
She coasted portly,
Through some sort of sorting.
Mingling with each man,
Married, taken, and single,
"It's your lucky day" was her
Icebreaking jingle.

The smoke was her veil,
And the booze helped her slide,
Dirty dancing her way
Right to my side.

Shamelessly, I glanced at her breasts,
But was yanked to attention
By the smell of her breath.
Her hair was mess.
Just like the rest of her body,
From her lipstick on sloppy,
To her knees so knobby.

My defenses were down
From hours of clowning around.
And she sensed I was a victim
Of my own blurry vision.
So she laid it on thick
By speaking in tongues.
Her words rolled off her tongue,
Then flung and stuck to me
Like elephant dung.

After last call
She followed me home.
Her motorcycle revving,
And her ready for fun.

And she got it!

Sunrise blurred her shape
In the distance.
She was gone before I knew.
I thought of last night's mischief,
And it wasn't clear
Who had gotten the better of who.